THE HEALING BREATH

THE HEALING BREATH

A JOURNEY BEYOND LOSS AND TRAUMA

JODY ELLIOTT

To Jeff, whose memory I carry with every breath.

To my loving family — my wife and my two boys — thank you for being my anchor and my inspiration every single day.

And to my parents, for their strength and love that have shaped me in ways words can't capture.

CONTENTS

INTRODUCTION

For the longest time, I thought breathwork sounded like another buzzword from wellness culture. I imagined meditative chants, the scent of incense, and vague promises about "finding inner peace." To be honest, the idea that something as simple as breathing could help with real problems—like anxiety, grief, or just the weight of day-to-day life—sounded like complete bullshit. I mean, we're breathing all the time, right? How could just doing it differently change anything?

I'll say it now: I'm not a fan of the word "mindfulness"—it's so overused that it's practically lost its meaning. In fact, this is the only time you'll see it here.

But life has a way of humbling you, especially when the usual methods of coping start to crack under the weight of what you've been holding back. Years of keeping emotions in check, staying strong, and holding on in silence can create a kind of pressure you don't even realize is there—until it starts to surface in unexpected ways. Anxiety, sleepless nights, and moments of feeling disconnected from everything, even from yourself. Those moments are like small signs, whispering that something isn't quite right.

I stumbled onto breathwork almost by accident. It wasn't part of some grand plan to heal or a quest to find enlightenment. I just heard about it in passing—meditation chats and books that mentioned it casually, like a side note. And yet, something about the idea stuck with me. The more I heard, the more I began to wonder: could something as simple as breathing really make a difference?

At first, my skepticism was strong. But it only took a few honest attempts for me to feel the impact—a weight lifting from deep inside, where I didn't even realize there was an issue. It wasn't just the relief; it was a sense of connection to myself that I hadn't felt in years. And that's when it clicked: breathwork wasn't about mystical promises or esoteric rituals. It was about getting back to something fundamental—something we all have but often forget to use.

Now, if you're reading this, you're probably open-minded to alternative solutions. And I encourage you to keep that open mind, because breathwork isn't about the simple act of breathing; it's in the techniques and the willingness to let them work. It may take a few tries, just as it did for me, but it works for so many people that it's likely to work for you too.

In today's world, where solutions are packaged in pills and endless distractions keep us from facing what's beneath the surface, breathwork offers an alternative. It's not a cure-all, and it's not magic, but it's something you can do at home, with no tools and no appointments—just you and your breath. And maybe, for those struggling with anxiety, grief, or the weight of unresolved emotions, that's where the real magic lies.

This book isn't just about breathwork techniques. It's about acknowledging the experiences that shape us, embracing the messiness of healing, and finding simple, practical ways to live a little lighter. If there's one thing I've learned, it's that we all have the power to reclaim our own stories. And sometimes, all it takes is learning how to breathe through the tough parts.

———

Throughout this book, you'll find small breathing prompts designed to help you pause and connect with the practice as you read. Think of them as checkpoints—moments to take a deep breath, reset, and let the ideas settle. These prompts are here to remind you that breathwork isn't just something to read about; it's something you can experience, right here, in real time. Keep an eye out for them as you go along.

CHAPTER 1
THE LAST NIGHT

Take a deep breath in… Hold for a moment, and then slowly let it go. As you exhale, allow yourself to arrive here, fully present. Let each breath ground you, preparing you for the journey ahead.

Thirty days before I blew out the candles on my fifth birthday cake, my fifteen-year-old brother was killed in a hit-and-run accident. He was walking home from a football game on the night after Halloween. On a rural, two-lane road, someone hit him with their car and dragged his body over two miles. To this day, the driver is still unknown.

I don't remember what I did last Tuesday, but I remember that night almost like stepping back into it—maybe not every detail, but the feelings as clear as if they'd just happened. I can slip right back into my little body, hearing the quiet hum of the crickets outside and the soft ticking of the kitchen clock. Dad sat in his usual spot on the couch, stoic as ever, his gaze lost in some thought only he knew. He was the kind of man who spoke more in gestures than words, a steady presence that anchored our family in his quiet way. Mom, on the other hand, was always laughing, the kind of woman whose voice filled every corner of the room. But that night, she seemed quieter too, her easygoing warmth somehow dimmed, almost as if she sensed the coming weight.

I remember the weight of the Knight Rider car in my small hands, the smooth plastic cool against my skin. The excitement bubbled in my chest as I watched my brother lift the T-shaped launcher, his face bright with a grin. The soft click of the pieces snapping together was like a promise, a pact between us.

"Just like on TV, right?" he said, his voice warm with amusement.

I nodded eagerly, my fingers tightening around my new treasure. For a moment, the world narrowed to just us, crouched on the linoleum kitchen floor, building dreams out of plastic and imagination.

My brother had grinned when he saw me clutching the box, excitement all over my face. He sat down beside me on the floor, showing me how to set up the T-shaped launcher, something a bit too technical for my 5-year-old dexterity, lining everything up just right.

When he stood to leave, I tugged at his hand, not ready to let the magic end. "C'mon, just one more time," I pleaded, hope straining in my voice.

He looked down at me, his smile softening into something more tender. Ruffling my hair, he made a vow: "Tomorrow, buddy. We'll race them first thing."

I didn't know then that tomorrow would never come, not in the way I expected. That his promise, whispered in the golden glow of our living room, would be the last he'd ever make to me. If I had known, would I have held on a little tighter? Would I have found the words to make him stay, just a moment longer?

But life rarely gives us such warnings. Instead, it hands us these small, perfect instances, fragile as spun glass, and trusts us to hold them close in the years to come.

The phone rang sometime after he left, I'm assuming sometime after midnight, slicing through the silence like a cold blade.

I remember Dad's voice staying steady as he listened, calm but somehow weighted with confusion. I couldn't hear my mom's voice on the other end, but I imagine him trying to console her, his quiet tone offering support the only way he knew. The call felt short, almost too short, like a moment that barely happened but changed everything. Then, in the dim light of our home, Dad took quick, quiet steps back to the bedroom and started getting me dressed. His hands worked fast, a mix of softness and urgency in his touch, as though time mattered in a way I couldn't understand.

Children know more than adults realize, and even at five, I sensed something was off. His movements were calm but not relaxed, his body language carrying a tension that filled the air around us. I watched him closely, searching his face for answers as he tucked my arms into my jacket and pulled on my shoes. There was no explanation, no comforting words—just the quiet hum of his urgency, a feeling in the air that made my small chest tighten with an unfamiliar dread. Part of me wanted to ask, but the other part just wanted to stay quiet and let him guide me.

The car ride is a blur. I'm the kind of person who can fall asleep within seconds as a passenger, and as a five-year-old, exhaustion and the weight of the late hour made it impossible to stay awake. I drifted in and out, barely aware of the road, the night, and the world outside. The last familiar sounds were my dad's voice and the feeling of being tucked into my seat, as though that routine could shield me from the strangeness of it all.

It was when we arrived that the memories become sharper, clearer, as though my mind recognized the weight of the moment even through my tiredness. We didn't go inside the police station; at least, it never felt that way. It felt as though we stood under a covered porch or perhaps an entryway surrounded by glass, with sterile light casting harsh shadows and making the air feel heavy. I remember the stillness as we walked up, my dad gently guiding me toward my mom and an officer who stood nearby, looking almost as lost as I felt.

My mother was crying in a way I had never heard before. It was a sound that cut through the quiet, one that no words could capture. I could feel her grief even though I didn't understand it, a force that settled in the air and weighed down every breath. I didn't know what was wrong, but I hated being there, hated the sterile lights and the thick, unspoken tension that filled the space around us. The officer's silence only added to the strangeness, like he didn't know how to comfort her or what to say to me. All I wanted in that moment was to disappear, to escape back to the familiar, wooded surroundings of home, a world where nothing this heavy could reach us.

Mom kept pressing him for answers, her voice quivering with desperation. "Who would do this?" she asked, looking for something, anything, that could explain the tragedy. "How could they just…?" She couldn't finish, her voice breaking as she tried to comprehend something beyond words. Her questions came out in bursts, one after another, each one met with the same silent gaze from the officer. He would shift his weight, glancing down, unable to meet her eyes for long, his own discomfort only deepening the silence.

"I need to know who did this," she insisted, her voice low but intense, as if the answers would somehow bring him back. But each time she asked, the officer's face remained expressionless, his eyes lowering as he gently shook his head, unable to offer anything concrete. He kept repeating, "We're doing everything we can," but the words felt empty, too formal to bring her any real comfort.

I watched her, feeling the sharpness in her voice, the urgency in her questions, each one an attempt to grasp something that kept slipping away. Her grief was raw, the kind I had never seen before, and it cut through the night's quiet, filling the sterile air with a heaviness that made my chest ache. I hated being there, hated the way her voice sounded—broken, almost pleading—and the way the officer's silence offered nothing back. I wanted to escape, to run away from the scene unfolding before me, but I felt rooted to the spot, as if by witnessing it, I could somehow make sense of what I was feeling.

My dad tried to comfort my mom, his arm around her shoulders, and I remember watching them, feeling that dread deepen. Children are perceptive, often more than we give them credit for, and even though I was only five, I knew enough to feel afraid. Every instinct told me to turn away, to avoid seeing whatever this was, but even as I drifted in and out of sleep, the weight of it pressed into me, like a puzzle piece that didn't fit but couldn't be ignored.

Now, as a father myself, I understand that awareness even more. My own five-year-old is as curious and sensitive as I was. He notices the smallest changes in my expressions, the slightest shifts in my mood. Sometimes, if I'm lost in thought, he'll ask me about the face I'm making—even when I don't feel like I'm making one. Children see everything; they pick up on our body language, our energy, in ways that are both innocent and profound. Knowing this, I realize how much I truly felt that night, the weight I carried without ever understanding why.

If I could reach back to that moment, I'd pull my younger self close and shield him from the sterile lights and heavy air, from the sounds of my mother's grief and the uncertainty that pressed into every corner. Now, I would do anything to keep my son from feeling that kind of dread, that instinct to escape and hide, even though he doesn't yet know what it is to want to run from something you can't explain.

That night was the beginning of a journey I didn't know I would carry my whole life. It was the moment a piece of me went quiet, a piece of my childhood that would never fully return. Over the years, I'd spend countless hours wondering what it meant to lose someone who meant everything, trying to find ways to fill the empty spaces he left behind. And eventually, I'd search for ways to breathe through it, to find a way to let go just enough to keep moving forward.

CHAPTER 2
HORNS ON MOSES

We were the last house on a dead-end road bearing my mother's family name. A mile down that road, at the opposite end, stood a small country church where I spent many Sunday mornings. While religion held little interest for me, I dutifully lowered my head with the congregation. The people were nice, some of the songs catchy, but, honestly, I was most drawn by the chance to ride my bike—or later, my dirt bike—that far from home.

After high school, I earned a scholarship to a Christian college, where a few Bible classes were required. I enrolled in Old Testament History, and for the first time, I encountered the hidden complexities of translation. I realized how fragile the chain of meaning is, where even a small mistranslation can send ripples through centuries of understanding. One famous example stuck with me: Michelangelo's statue of Moses, where Moses, due to a single mistranslation, was given horns instead of a radiant face.

In the original Hebrew text, the word *karan* described Moses' face as "radiant" after he descended from Mount Sinai. But when the Bible was translated into Latin for the Vulgate edition, the translator, Saint Jerome, chose the Latin word *cornuta*, which means "horned," instead of something closer to "radiated" or "shone." With that single choice, Moses was transformed from a man glowing with divine light to a figure with literal horns sprouting from his head. This error, though seemingly minor, became deeply embedded in Western art and culture.

Michelangelo later sculpted Moses with horns on his head, and this depiction—based solely on that mistranslation—has persisted for centuries, shaping how many viewed the figure of Moses. A single misstep in language altered not just Moses' appearance in art, but it also left a lasting mark on how people understood his character. To this day, that version of Moses with horns stands as a reminder of how a slight shift in words can permanently alter the world's perception, embedding an error that can take on a life of its own.

Michelangelo's Moses courtesy of Livioandronico2013
(https://commons.wikimedia.org/wiki/File:
Michelangelo's_Moses_(Rome).jpg)

It was eye-opening to consider that almost everything I had ever read, every phrase, was vulnerable to the same risks of error or misunderstanding. Language, I learned, is a shaky bridge at best. And yet, language is all we have. No matter how complex or rich our vocabulary, every experience is a bit ineffable, something that words can only approach, never truly capture. Try to describe the taste of chocolate, for instance. We might reach for words like "bitterness" or "sweetness," or maybe "smooth" and "rich." But those words only skim the surface. They don't capture the way chocolate melts slowly on the tongue, releasing a complex mix of flavors, or the faint hint of something earthy and roasted that sits just beneath the sweetness. They don't evoke the warmth it brings, the way a single piece can lift a mood, stir nostalgia, or calm a craving. Language can point to these sensations, but it can't bottle them. What words can truly describe that depth of flavor and the way it wraps around the senses?

Each attempt to describe it feels like reaching toward something just out of grasp, a shadow of the experience. In that gap between what we sense and what we say, there's a kind of silence, a wordless understanding that can't be shared—only felt. Words fall short, leaving us with a reminder of their limits, a quiet space where language fails and the experience simply is.

Reflecting on it now, the irony isn't lost on me that I'm relying on these very words—the ones I find so limited—to try to convey my experience to you. There's a strange contradiction in knowing that while language often fails to reach the heart of an experience, here I am, using it to try and paint a picture, to fill in the gaps, hoping it might resonate with you. Words are clumsy, often inadequate, but they're all I have to bridge the gap between my reality and yours.

I thought back to my childhood and realized how strongly I felt that silence after my brother died. I was five. The people around me tried to explain what had happened, why everyone seemed sad or somber, but I didn't have the words to connect with their explanations or with my own grief. And so, I carried an unnamed weight that no one could help me lift. I think many people, as they grow older, continue to carry that unspoken weight because language, with all its complexities, can't reach what's wordless.

My parents did their best to protect me from further loss. They put restrictions on what I could do, on how far I could go. I wasn't allowed to play football; later, when I got my driver's license, I subconsciously drove with a caution that felt baked into my very bones. The trauma had embedded itself as a kind of wordless caution, something I couldn't name, let alone explain.

Part of the burden, I realize now, was the absence of words. I didn't know how to ask for help, to even identify what I was feeling. That isolation of unspoken feelings is hard to explain to someone who hasn't lived through it. Words can let us down by being clumsy, too small to hold our pain. Or worse, words from others can feel inadequate or even dismissive, leaving us more isolated than before.

Take a deep, calming breath in… and exhale slowly. Let yourself find peace in the space between the words, holding onto what resonates and letting go of what doesn't.

My mom turned to words to cope. She spent hours writing rhyming poems, assembling fragments of feeling into lines that gave her some sense of control. I remember her reading a few at church; I thought it was silly back then, but now I can see the power in that practice. Language, however flawed, was her tool. It gave her something to hold on to when everything else was slipping away. I didn't have that. I carried my grief and confusion quietly, as if my silence could somehow bridge the gap between what I felt and what others could understand.

It took me years to realize that, like my mother, I could find release in words—even if they only circled the truth without touching it. Language can be a rough, imperfect tool, but by giving form to thoughts, it lets us see them clearly, as something outside ourselves. It's almost therapeutic, the process of putting words to what's unspoken, even if we know those words won't get us all the way there.

Language, with its limitations and gaps, is both a friend and a failing. Words like "grief" or "loss" become placeholders, markers for something much deeper. We can never fully convey our experiences, but by trying, we reach across the silence. For me, the struggle to bridge that silence has shaped how I see words, not as answers but as guides. Even now, I know that each phrase, each attempt to describe my past, falls short. But with every line, I come a little closer to making peace with the spaces in between.

Eventually, though, I realized that words alone weren't enough to make sense of the weight I carried. After seeing how language could mislead or fall short, I started to wonder if I was looking in the wrong places for comfort. Maybe grief couldn't be untangled in conversations or verses, as my mother had tried to do. The answers I needed might be somewhere else—beyond words, outside the stories we tell ourselves to cope.

So, I began to look elsewhere, curious to see if relief could be found in silence or in the simple act of being. I searched for understanding in moments when language wasn't expected or required. Sometimes, this meant spending time outdoors, where thoughts came and went without needing to be spoken. Other times, it meant sitting alone, listening to the space around me, hoping that something—anything—would bring a sense of calm beyond what words could offer.

The failure of language to capture what I felt wasn't just frustrating; it was freeing. It was as if, in realizing the limitations of words, I could finally allow myself to explore other ways of coping. I began to realize that maybe healing didn't require definitions or explanations. Perhaps it lay in something as simple and natural as breathing, in letting go enough to feel whatever surfaced without needing to explain it.

In the end, words failed, but the silence between them became a space to simply be—a place where I didn't have to explain my grief or make sense of it. It was in that silence, where words didn't reach, that I began to find the relief I had been seeking.

CHAPTER 3
SHADOWS IN THE SILENCE

ountry people love folklore. Where I grew up, the old stories come alive, carried on the voices of family members, neighbors, and friends. It's like folklore fills in the blanks where facts don't, especially when you live in places where the outside world hardly intrudes. The mountains and woods around us are barriers and borders—keeping us in and keeping everything else out. That isolation gives rise to beliefs that are as real to folks around here as any scientific proof. And it's my theory that this lack of outside voices, of new ideas or explanations, is exactly why folklore is so deeply rooted.

People here don't just hear ghost stories; they know them. You don't have to go far to find someone who's sure they've encountered something—a spirit, a 'haint,' or some other presence in the shadows. And I get it; I was right there with them. As a kid, I was pretty convinced that ghosts were as real as my own two hands. Every bump in the night, every eerie silence was proof that there was more out there. Some of that belief came from ghost stories and Hollywood, sure, but a big part of it came from wanting to believe.

After my brother died, I'd have given anything to see him

again, even if it was just a flicker in the corner of my eye. I wanted that so badly that it didn't take much to convince me that he might be lingering around. It wasn't just me, though. The belief in ghosts was nearly universal around here. There's a sort of comfort in thinking our loved ones never truly leave us, that maybe they're just beyond our reach but close enough to show up if the conditions are right.

That's the strange thing about these parts—people are cautious about what they believe, but they're also oddly willing to believe in something if it offers a glimmer of hope or explanation. It's a curious balance. We inherit both skepticism and superstition, passed down from our Scots-Irish ancestors who brought with them a peculiar mix of religious fervor, wariness, and belief in the supernatural. We're skeptical of outsiders and new ideas, but we cling to old stories like lifelines.

Pause here and take a gentle, grounding breath. Let the breath anchor you, holding space for the stories we tell ourselves to bring comfort and connection.

In some ways, it feels like living with one foot in two worlds—resistant to being fooled by anything new but holding onto beliefs that haven't budged in centuries. And for me, that tension is where I sit, too. I'm cautious of anything that feels like "woo-woo" nonsense, but I also feel that itch to believe, the pull of wanting there to be more than what I can see or understand. It's a funny contradiction, and it's one I've carried my whole life.

Then there was Vic Tandy. Now, Vic wasn't from my neck of the woods. He was a British engineer and fencer, of all things, but he found himself haunted in his own way. He worked in a lab that some folks claimed was haunted, though I'd bet he didn't pay much mind to that. One night, though, something changed. While working late, he felt a chill run down his spine, his neck hairs prickling as if something was watching him. And in his peripheral vision, he saw a strange, gray shape—an apparition, maybe. But when he turned to face it, there was nothing there. It rattled him enough to make him start questioning what was happening.

But Vic was a man of science, not the type to get carried away. He set out to understand what had happened, and the next day he noticed his fencing blade, which he'd left in a vise, vibrating on its own. Eventually, he figured it out: his lab had an extractor fan that hummed along at 19Hz. That frequency sits just at the edge of what our ears can pick up, too low for us to hear but strong enough to mess with our minds. Sound at that frequency can make you feel uneasy, even panicked, and it just so happens that 19Hz also causes a slight resonance in our eyeballs. That resonance was enough to make Vic think he saw something—a shadowy "ghost" hanging just outside his direct vision. Once the fan was turned off, the haunting vanished. The ghost was nothing more than a vibration.

That story stuck with me. It showed how much we take on faith without even realizing it. Here's the thing: we trust what we can see and hear, but Vic's experience made me wonder how reliable that trust really is. If a sound wave can make us feel like we're in the presence of something unearthly, or a vibration can trick our eyes into seeing a ghost, what else are we being fooled by? Our senses, the tools we use to navigate the world, are far from perfect. They only give us a glimpse of reality, not the full picture.

Let's talk about sound for a second. Sound is just vibrations moving through the air, and human hearing spans from about 20Hz to 20,000Hz. Below 20Hz, there's infrasound, which we can't consciously hear. But that doesn't mean it doesn't affect us. Infrasound can create feelings of dread, make our stomachs turn, or send shivers down our spines—all without us realizing why. It's like there's a frequency for fear, hidden just beyond our perception. Sounds at this range come from things like earthquakes, thunder, or the growl of a big predator, and some scientists think we evolved to feel these sounds as a warning, a signal to be on high alert. It's a survival mechanism embedded in our biology, lurking just out of reach but close enough to feel.

And it's not just sound; our sight works the same way. Just like with sound waves, we only see a narrow band of the light spectrum. Our eyes pick up light from around 400 to 700 nanometers, which is just a sliver of the electromagnetic spectrum. Beyond violet, there's ultraviolet light, and beyond red, there's infrared—both of which are invisible to us without special equipment. We might think we're seeing everything, but in reality, we're catching a fraction of what's out there. The rest of it—the colors and shapes beyond our visual range—is lost to us, hidden in plain sight.

When I think about Vic's ghost and what it represents, it pulls me deeper into a sort of skeptical wonder. His story reminds me that what we experience isn't necessarily what's real; it's just a slice of what's possible. Our senses give us enough to get by, but they're far from complete, and that realization taught me to be cautious. It taught me to question what I think I know, to be skeptical of the explanations that seem too simple. At the same time, though, it also opened me up to the unknown. If there's so much beyond our senses, who's to say what's really out there?

And that's the contradiction I wrestle with. On the one hand, knowing how easily we're fooled makes me doubt everything a little more. But on the other, it leaves room for mystery, for the possibility that there's more than what I can explain or understand. Growing up in a place where belief in ghosts was nearly universal, I can't quite shake the idea that maybe, just maybe, there's something beyond the veil. Not necessarily a haint or a spirit, but something that we're not yet equipped to sense.

For me, that tension—between skepticism and openness—is where I've landed. It's a balancing act between what I know and what I'm willing to believe. And in the end, it's made me more curious, not less. Because if I can only hear certain sounds, only see certain colors, then what else is out there, waiting just beyond my reach? How much of this world goes unseen, unheard, just out of range?

CHAPTER 4
FUMES

"True happiness is to enjoy the present without anxious dependence upon the future, not to amuse ourselves with either hopes or fears but to rest satisfied with what we have, which is sufficient, for he that is so wants nothing." -- Seneca

---

Growing up, my dad had a fascination with Chevrolets, turning each project into a ritual we'd share. But the trips to town weren't always just about getting car parts---they were an entryway to meet people like Gene, a man who somehow embodied a strange contentment in the present. Even as I grew older and learned more about his flaws, there was something about his carefree spirit that stuck with me.

Dad collected Chevy parts the way some people collect memories. His workshop, our big metal garage, overflowed with decommissioned refrigerators full of alternators, starters, and old tools. One morning, before I could grab cereal or catch my favorite Saturday cartoons—Teenage Mutant Ninja Turtles, clearly the best

—I found myself in the cab of his truck, heading to town to scavenge for more.

We pulled up in front of what looked like a row of storage units. Suddenly, a garage door opened like a magician's cape, releasing a thick cloud of paint overspray that floated out into the morning air. The acrid smell of chemicals stung my nostrils, and I could feel the fine mist settling on my skin. The man inside wore his acetone-drenched clothes and paint-streaked skin like badges of honor. He'd painted so many cars without a mask that his lungs seemed immune to the fumes. Though, let's be honest—he was probably just high as a kite, adding a little extra flair to each paint job. I remember standing outside, barely breathing, while he calmly smoked a cigarette and waited for the cloud to dissipate. Only then did he wave us in to begin the search for whatever car part my dad had his eye on that day.

Inside, a boat sat patiently under a thick shroud of dust and overspray. Dad and the painter began digging through boxes lining the left wall, their movements echoing in the stillness. As they worked, the boat cover was cast aside, and up from beneath it rose a man I'll never forget. To this day, I still don't know why in the hell Gene was sleeping in a boat in a makeshift paint booth—it was just one of those things you didn't question about him.

This was Gene: super skinny, with rough skin and a scraggly, short beard that looked like it grew more from habit than any conscious grooming. His face was all sharp angles and weary lines, as though life had weathered him one story at a time. And he had plenty of those. If his likeness had ever been turned into a Sesame Street muppet, he would have fit right in—his quirky, weathered look perfect for a puppet with a tale to tell. Gene was a compulsive exaggerator, a man whose stories grew with each telling. Once, he came by our house during a basketball game and couldn't leave until he'd told us he had "big money" on the game—knowing full well he hadn't bet a penny. But there was something endearing in his tales, as if stretching the truth let him feel larger than life, even just for a moment.

As I grew older, I began to realize that Gene's stories were often more fiction than fact. His tales, filled with wild claims and vivid details, seemed designed more for entertainment than truth. Over time, it became clear that his knack for embellishment was less about deception and more about creating a larger-than-life persona. The line between reality and the myths he crafted blurred so thoroughly that it was hard to tell where the real Gene ended and his stories began.

That day in the garage, Gene greeted us with the same gusto. From deep within his whiskery face spewed a whirlwind of thoughts, all tumbling out at once. He started by praising the comfort of the boat he'd apparently been sleeping in, then transitioned to last night's basketball scores, then something about a woman he once knew and the pain in his left knee. He was a hurricane of ideas and half-finished thoughts, all spoken as if they were the most important thing in the world. I couldn't take my eyes off him, wondering how much of his erratic energy was just Gene and how much might have been fueled by the fumes that seemed to cling to him like an old coat.

Despite his flaws, despite the lies that seemed to fill in the gaps of his life, Gene had a happiness that felt rare. He was a man who carried nothing with him, not even the burden of truth, yet he seemed genuinely glad to see us there that day. There was a freedom in him that I couldn't shake, as though he'd stumbled upon a secret most of us missed in the rush to be respectable or reliable.

In the months and years that followed, I'd spot Gene around town. He was still a nomad, always drifting, never settling. He didn't seem to have much of a home or a family he stayed close to, and word was he wasn't around for his kids. But he wore a smile like it was the only thing that mattered.

As I grew older, I learned that Gene's carefree spirit came at a cost. His drifting, his spontaneity, and his disregard for convention —qualities that made him so fascinating to observe—were likely sources of pain and disappointment for those closest to him. This realization tempered my admiration for Gene's lifestyle and made me grapple with the difficult question of how to find balance between personal fulfillment and the responsibilities we owe to others.

In a world that often equates success with academic achievements and financial stability, Gene stood out as a stark contrast. His lack of formal education and his simple, nomadic lifestyle seemed to defy the expectations of our community. Yet, there was a certain wisdom in his approach to life—a recognition that happiness and fulfillment could be found in the present moment, rather than in the constant pursuit of external markers of success. Gene's example challenged me to question my own assumptions about what it means to live a meaningful life.

Gene's presence became a reminder that true peace isn't about having everything—it's about finding joy in what you already have. As I grew older, I began to understand the wisdom in Gene's approach. He didn't need grand plans or material possessions to be content. He didn't dwell on what went wrong yesterday or worry about what might go wrong tomorrow. Instead, he relished each moment, each encounter, each conversation as if it were the only thing in the world. Maybe it is.

Breathe in for a count of four... hold for two... and exhale for six. Let each breath be a reminder of the simple, small moments that bring us back to ourselves.

Gene's life was a lesson in simplicity, something he demonstrated both in subtle moments and with all the absurdity you'd expect from him. Years after that meeting in the garage, he found himself in one of his legendary escapades. He'd been drunk driving and while in a parking lot when he collided with another car. Turns out, the owner of the other car was just as sloshed, stumbling out of a bar to inspect the damage. Instead of calling it in, the two of them shook hands on a wild plan: they'd re-enact the crash the next day when they were sober, for 'authenticity.' I shit you not.

And so, true to his word, Gene showed up the following day, barreling straight through the guy's front yard and slamming into that same car like he'd just time-traveled from the night before. As if that wasn't enough, he even pulled out broken taillights from his trunk that he'd salvaged, scattering them around to make the scene look real.

That was Gene. The same man who stretched the truth, swore on bets he'd never made, and barreled through life—fenders, tail-lights, and all. Somehow, for all the chaos he left in his wake, there was something strangely freeing about the way he lived in the moment, never once asking himself if there was a better way.

CHAPTER 5
THE SILENCE BETWEEN US

There Is An Empty Place

There are no words
that I can write
To tell just how
I feel tonight.
My heart is broken
half in two,
There's a hurt in my chest
that I never knew.

There's an empty chair
at my table now,
They say I have to get
used to it somehow.
But I think, I know
that will never be,
No one knows
what is inside of me.

There's an empty place
that no one can fill.
I can't forget
and I never will.
I guess only God
knows what is to be.
He took my precious
son from me.

Fifteen years old
now he's gone,
Left to die
on the road alone.
For all those years,
he was my sunshine.
I thank God
that he was mine.

He was always
my pride and joy.
Everyone said
he was a special boy.
I will never forget
the memories he left,
And no one knows
how I miss my Jeff.

\- A POEM BY MY MOTHER, WRITTEN
IN 1985

n my house, grief wasn't something we talked about—it was something we lived with, quietly and stubbornly, like a stray dog that just wouldn't leave. After my brother died, things seemed to go back to normal, at least from the outside. I still played with my toys, went to school, and watched cartoons on Saturday mornings. But even as life continued, there was an unspoken tension that lingered in the background.

My parents came from tough roots. Neither of them finished high school, but they knew how to survive. My mom was one of twelve kids, raised by a father who made and sold moonshine out of necessity. It wasn't glamorous, but it put food on the table. My dad's family was smaller, but they were no better off. He grew up in a household where being tough was the only way to make it through, and that hardness stayed with him. They were both practical, no-nonsense people who loved fiercely but didn't always know how to show it.

After my brother died, their grief showed itself in subtle ways. My dad had always been a beer drinker, but after my brother died, Friday nights turned into a ritual of drinking a bit more than usual. He never touched the hard stuff, but a case of beer would disappear by the end of the night. As a kid, I didn't think much of it, but looking back, I realize it was his way of coping. He couldn't talk about his pain, so he found a way to dull it instead.

Mom dealt with it differently. She left my brother's room exactly the way it was for years. His bed was always made, his clothes still hung in the closet, and his favorite jacket was draped over the back of his chair, like he might walk in any minute and grab it on his way out. Sometimes she'd swear she could still smell him in the house—a combination of sweat mixed with earthy musk, the lingering scent of deodorant, and sometimes the faint odor of stale socks or worn-in sneakers. They weren't the kind of people to believe in ghosts, but when she mentioned it, my dad would go quiet. He'd act like he didn't feel it, but I always thought he did. I think that silence of his gave her some small comfort, as if they both silently agreed to believe in that faint trace of him.

There was something about storms that always unsettled my dad, and they still do. I never knew if it was something that happened in his own childhood or just a nervous inclination, but he'd tense up every time thunderclouds rolled in. Our small house wasn't exactly built to last, and the trees surrounding us seemed like a threat during strong winds. My brother, despite only being fifteen, had a way of comforting both my parents during storms, reassuring them as if he were older than all of us. After he was gone, my mom would sometimes swear she felt his presence nearby whenever a storm passed through. She'd ask Dad if he felt it too, but he'd just go to another room, hiding his true feelings, never answering her question.

For me, the shift wasn't something I could put into words at the time, but I felt it all the same. My parents were loving, but there was a distance between us that hadn't been there before. It was as if we were all tiptoeing around something too fragile to touch. The house felt different, like it was holding its breath, waiting for something to break the spell.

Life carried on, but there were small changes that spoke to a deeper grief. Dad started spending more time in the garage, his hands deep in the engine of whatever truck he was fixing up. I'd sometimes sit on an overturned bucket, watching him work in silence, the steady clink of his tools and the low hum of the garage filling the space, with the smell of grease and metal hanging thick in the air. He never talked about my brother, and I didn't know how to ask, so we just shared those quiet hours together, each of us lost in our own thoughts.

After my brother died, Mom seemed quieter, her sadness lingering in small, almost imperceptible ways. She hadn't worked since I was born, but not long after, she took a job as a kindergarten assistant, filling her days with other people's children. At home, she moved through routines with a new kind of distance, her laughter a bit more rare and her energy softened. She'd still cook our meals and keep the house running, but there was a heaviness that settled into her every move, as if she were carrying an invisible weight that none of us dared to talk about.

My presence in the house probably helped them more than I realized. After losing Jeff, the silence must have been unbearable at times. Even if I couldn't fill the space my brother left behind, I gave them something to hold onto. I was a reminder that they hadn't lost everything, and maybe that was enough to keep them moving forward.

The funny thing about grief is that it doesn't always look the way you expect. It's not all tears and outbursts. Sometimes, it's just a quiet heaviness that hangs in the air, a weight you can't see but always feel. Looking back, I realize that unspoken pain shaped my childhood in ways I didn't understand until much later. It taught me to keep my own feelings hidden, to avoid making waves or saying the wrong thing. It wasn't until years later, when I started to confront my own grief, that I began to see just how deeply that silence had affected me.

For all their hardness, my parents did the best they could with what they had. They were trying to protect me, even if they didn't know how to protect themselves. And in their silence, I think there was a kind of love too—a love that tried to shield me from the worst of their pain, even if it meant never really talking about it.

It's strange to think about now, but those small moments of shared silence, of sitting in the garage with my dad or listening to my mom clean the house, are some of my strongest memories from that time. They're moments that, at the time, didn't feel like anything special. But now, I see them for what they were—small acts of resilience, quiet ways of holding on to what we had left.

As I grew older, I started to understand that the silence wasn't just about the loss of my brother. It was about all the unspoken pain that lingered in our house, tucked away behind closed doors and buried beneath layers of toughness. Over the years, the silence and grief faded, softening around the edges, but it was never really gone. It became a quiet undercurrent in our lives, a weight I carried with me, pressing it down until it grew too heavy to ignore.

CHAPTER 6
THE THINGS WE CARRY

Trauma is a strange thing. It's not just a memory or an event—it's a weight you carry, one that settles deep into your bones and finds ways to make itself known, even when you're not consciously thinking about it. In some ways, it's like an invisible wound that never fully heals. You can't see it, but you feel its effects in everything you do.

Neuroscientists have found that trauma rewires the brain. When we experience something overwhelming, the amygdala—our brain's emotional command center—becomes hyperactive, while the hippocampus, responsible for processing memories, can actually shrink. It's as if the brain creates a special filing system for these overwhelming experiences, storing them differently from ordinary memories. That's why trauma survivors often experience flashbacks that feel as vivid as the original event—the memory hasn't been properly filed away as "past."

Psychologists describe trauma as a disruption in the mind's ability to process an event. It's like the brain hits a roadblock and can't figure out how to move forward. The nervous system goes into overdrive, either locking into a state of high alert or retreating into numbness. The fight-or-flight response—meant to protect you from immediate threats—gets stuck in the "on" position, even when the danger is long gone.

Research shows that trauma doesn't just live in our minds—it leaves its mark on our bodies, too. Dr. Bessel van der Kolk, a pioneering trauma researcher, describes this in his book *The Body Keeps the Score*. Even when we think we've moved past something, our bodies remember. Heart rate variability changes, muscle tension patterns shift, and even our immune systems are affected. It's as if every cell holds a piece of the story.

Over time, this unresolved response can manifest in countless ways: anxiety, depression, chronic stress, or physical ailments like headaches and muscle tension. Studies have shown that people with unresolved trauma are more likely to develop autoimmune conditions, chronic pain, and cardiovascular problems. The body's stress response system becomes dysregulated, leading to what researchers call "allostatic load"—the wear and tear of chronic stress on the body.

In children, trauma often expresses itself indirectly, through behaviors and coping mechanisms that might seem unrelated. Kids can't articulate complex emotions the way adults can, so they find ways to adapt. They might withdraw, become overly compliant, or act out in seemingly random ways. Recent studies in developmental neuroscience reveal that childhood trauma can even alter gene expression through epigenetic modification—the trauma leaves its mark on DNA, potentially affecting future generations.

In my case, I think humor became my way of handling the parts of life that were too heavy to deal with directly. Laughter was something I learned early on. My mom, for all her hardness, had a sharp sense of humor. She could find something to laugh about in almost any situation, and her laugh was this big, contagious thing that made the whole room light up. Even in the darkest times, she'd find a way to crack a joke, her laughter keeping the darkness at bay. When words weren't enough to carry the weight, humor stepped in to do the heavy lifting.

As a kid, I didn't think of humor as a coping mechanism; it was just part of life, part of who I was. I loved making people laugh, loved the sound of it, and the way it could turn a heavy moment into something lighter. I didn't know it then, but it was more than just a way to connect—it was a way to protect myself from the things I didn't want to feel. I only saw it for what it was years later, and over time, it became part of my identity.

Psychologists label this behavior a "defense mechanism," and humor is a particularly common one. It's a way of reframing pain or fear into something more manageable, a way of taking control of a situation that feels out of your hands. And in small doses, it's actually pretty healthy. Laughter releases endorphins, reduces stress, and creates a sense of connection with others. But like any defense mechanism, it has its limits. If humor becomes your only way of dealing with emotions, it can keep you from truly processing what's going on beneath the surface.

For me, humor became a reflex. When someone made a cutting remark, I'd fire back with a witty comeback before the sting had a chance to set in. When things got awkward or uncomfortable, I'd make a joke to defuse the situation. And when I was feeling down, I'd do everything I could to make other people laugh, as if their laughter could somehow drown out my own sadness. It wasn't something I did consciously—I just knew it worked. Over time, I've become pretty damn good at it.

Looking back, I can see how that early trauma shaped the way I moved through the world. It wasn't just the big, obvious things like avoiding conversations about my brother or feeling a sense of unease when I saw an accident on the side of the road. It was the small, subtle ways it influenced my behavior, the unspoken rules I had internalized without even realizing it. Don't get too close to people. Don't let your guard down. Keep things light and funny, and maybe you won't have to deal with what's really going on.

What we now know about trauma recovery is that it requires a multifaceted approach. Traditional talk therapy helps, but so do movement, art, and other forms of expression that engage the body and the unconscious mind. Therapies like EMDR (Eye Movement Desensitization and Reprocessing) and somatic experiencing work directly with the nervous system, helping release trapped trauma responses and create new neural pathways.

But the problem with using humor as a shield is that it only works for so long. The things you're trying to keep at bay eventually find a way to slip through the cracks. In my case, that weight of unresolved grief and unspoken pain made itself known in other ways. I had trouble forming deep connections, always keeping people at a safe distance without realizing I was doing it. I'd find myself feeling restless and uneasy, as if there was something gnawing at me that I couldn't quite put my finger on.

The concept of *post-traumatic growth* has gained attention in recent years—the idea that trauma, while devastating, can also be a catalyst for profound personal transformation. Research shows that some survivors develop increased resilience, deeper relationships, and a stronger sense of purpose. It's not that the trauma goes away, but rather that we learn to carry it differently, to integrate it into our story in a way that allows for both acknowledgment of the pain and the possibility of growth.

I still love humor. I love the way it can turn a heavy moment into something bearable, the way it can make people feel lighter, even if only for a little while. There's something powerful about seeing someone smile, knowing you put that light in their eyes, even when your own heart feels heavy. It's not just a coping mechanism—it's a way of connecting, of finding a shared moment of relief in a world that can feel too heavy at times.

Understanding trauma through this lens—as both a psychological and physiological experience—helps explain why recovery isn't just about "getting over it" or "moving on." It's about learning to regulate a dysregulated system, about creating new neural pathways alongside the old ones, about finding ways to feel safe in a body that has learned to expect danger.

But as I grew older, I started to understand that laughter wasn't always enough. There were things I needed to face, things I had buried so deep that I didn't even realize they were there. And while humor could deflect those feelings for a while, it couldn't make them go away. It took years for me to see that part of myself clearly, to recognize that the jokes and the laughter were sometimes a way of hiding the things I wasn't ready to deal with.

Breathe in deeply, filling your lungs… and exhale fully. Allow this breath to create space for both laughter and healing in your journey.

The thing about trauma is that it doesn't just disappear over time. It settles in, becomes a part of you, and finds ways to shape your life in ways you might not even be aware of. It influences your thoughts, your behaviors, and your relationships, like a shadow that's always there, just out of sight. But with understanding comes the possibility of change—not erasing the past, but creating new pathways alongside it, finding ways to carry our stories with both honesty and hope.

CHAPTER 7
SOMEWHERE BETWEEN BREATHS

When it comes to dealing with trauma, people have all sorts of ways to cope. Some turn to humor, like I did, while others seek solace in routines or find distraction in their work. Some numb their pain with substances—alcohol, drugs, or even food—trying to drown out the noise of old wounds. And then there are those who throw themselves into their passions, hoping that if they stay busy enough, they won't have to face what's been gnawing at them all along.

> Now, as time begins its healing for the mother, there is a sudden awareness, or awakening, for five-year-old Jody

Clipping from a 1985 news article. The words 'awareness' and 'awakening' feel strangely prophetic

For years, I thought I was doing fine. I wasn't one to dwell on the past or wallow in emotions. My life moved forward, and so did I, at least on the surface. But there were moments when that old restlessness would creep in, a feeling that something wasn't quite right. I wasn't falling apart, but I wasn't whole either. The more I ignored it, the heavier it seemed to get.

Looking back, I realize how easy it is to convince ourselves that we've moved past something simply because we don't think about it daily. But grief, trauma—these things don't just disappear. They simmer beneath the surface, influencing our decisions, our moods, and our interactions in ways we often don't notice until something brings them bubbling back up.

I never thought I'd be the kind of person to explore something like breathwork. I grew up in a world where emotions weren't exactly discussed, let alone processed. If someone had told me a few years ago that focused breathing sessions could help release decades of buried grief, I probably would've laughed in their face. I was skeptical of anything that smelled even remotely "woo-woo," and the idea of sitting still and breathing my problems away seemed more than a little ridiculous.

But the thing about carrying old pain is that it doesn't go away on its own. You can push it down, laugh it off, or distract yourself with work, but it finds a way to bubble up, even when you least expect it. For me, that reckoning came in my 40s. I didn't hit rock bottom or have a dramatic breakdown. It was more like a slow realization that I wasn't as okay as I thought I was. It started with little things—trouble sleeping, feeling on edge for no reason, moments of irritability that seemed to come out of nowhere. I could feel something trying to surface, and humor wasn't enough to keep it at bay anymore. I needed something different, something I didn't even have a name for yet.

· · ·

That's when I stumbled across breathwork. I wasn't searching for it, but in some roundabout way, it found me. It started with a casual conversation and led to a friend's health business event, where he invited me to try a breathwork session he was offering for a few of his employees. It was a small group, and something about that setting made me feel comfortable enough to give it a real shot. Maybe it was the familiarity of being around people I knew, or maybe I was just ready to try something different.

The first couple of times, I still felt like an imposter. I wasn't sure what I was supposed to be doing or if I was doing it "right." All I knew was that I was sitting there, trying to focus on my breath while a small, skeptical voice in the back of my head kept whispering, *This is ridiculous.* I went through the motions, breathing in deeply, holding, and then exhaling slowly. It felt mechanical, almost forced, and when nothing significant happened, my skepticism only deepened.

But on a third attempt, at another later work event, something clicked. By then, I was tired of feeling like I was holding back, tired of questioning myself at every turn. My social anxiety usually kept me from letting go, always making me worry about what others thought, even when I was alone. But in that small group, something shifted. I threw caution to the wind and gave it everything I had. I stopped trying to control the experience and let myself breathe without holding back. Looking back, I realize the environment played a crucial role—lying down instead of sitting and the perfectly chosen music created the space I needed to finally let go.

That's when I felt it—a stillness in my mind that I'd never quite reached through meditation. It wasn't a forced stillness but a natural quiet that settled in as I surrendered to the breath. For the first time, I wasn't fighting the experience or trying to mold it into something specific. I was just breathing, and it felt like I was finally doing something right.

Pause here, taking a slow inhale and exhale, as you let whatever thoughts are present settle and observe them without judgment.

After that third session, I knew there was something to this practice. It wasn't just about calming my mind—it was about creating space for emotions I hadn't fully processed, emotions that had been lurking just below the surface for years. Breathwork wasn't a magic cure, but it was a doorway, a way to access the parts of myself that I'd been avoiding.

Not long after, I found a breathwork teacher who approached the practice in a way that resonated with me. Breathwork teachers come in all varieties, and this one was practical, no-nonsense, and clear. He didn't throw around vague spiritual language or promise life-changing results. Instead, he explained the science behind the practice—how controlled breathing could influence the nervous system, helping to shift the body from a state of "fight or flight" into "rest and digest."

Pause here and take a few natural breaths. Feel the rise and fall of your chest, acknowledging the many ways we try to navigate our experiences.

There's a physiological basis to breathwork that appealed to my skeptical side. When you breathe deeply and deliberately, you stimulate the vagus nerve, a key player in regulating your body's stress response. By activating the vagus nerve, you can lower your heart rate, reduce cortisol levels, and essentially tell your body that it's safe to let go. It's a simple concept, but it has powerful effects. Studies have shown that regular breathwork can help reduce anxiety, improve focus, and even lower blood pressure. For someone like me, who spent years feeling like my mind was always racing, the idea that something as basic as breathing could calm that chaos was almost too good to be true.

The more I practiced, the more I realized that breathwork wasn't just a tool for managing stress; it was a way to connect with myself on a deeper level. Each session became a journey inward, peeling back layers of old pain, forgotten memories, and long-held beliefs about who I was and what I could handle.

I began to notice changes outside of the breathwork sessions too. Conversations with friends felt a bit lighter, my reactions to stressful situations weren't as intense, and the constant hum of anxiety that had become my background noise started to fade. I wasn't "fixed," but I was more present, more aware of the undercurrents that had been steering my life for so long.

One of the most profound realizations came during a particularly intense session. As I lay there, breathing deeply, I felt a wave of emotion rise within me. It started as a tightness in my chest, then grew into an overwhelming sense of grief. Tears streamed down my face, and for the first time in years, I allowed myself to fully feel the weight of my loss. I wasn't just mourning the past; I was releasing it, breath by breath.

It wasn't all smooth sailing, though. There were sessions where nothing seemed to happen, and I left feeling frustrated and skeptical all over again. But even those sessions taught me something important: the process isn't about forcing outcomes. It's about showing up, being present, and trusting that whatever needs to surface will do so in its own time.

Breathwork became a practice of patience and surrender, a way to gently coax my body and mind into letting go of the armor they'd built up over the years. And in that letting go, I found a kind of freedom I hadn't known was possible—a freedom to feel, to heal, and to breathe deeply into the life that was waiting for me on the other side of my pain.

Important Note on Breathwork Safety

While breathwork can be a powerful tool for emotional and physical release, it's important to acknowledge that not every technique is suitable for everyone. Before diving into more intense breathwork practices, please consider any preexisting health conditions you may have. For instance, if you have a history of heart issues, breathing difficulties, or conditions like epilepsy, consult a healthcare provider before engaging in intensive sessions. Breathwork can induce strong physical responses like dizziness, tingling, or even a sense of lightheadedness. If at any time you feel overwhelmed or uncomfortable, take a break or try a gentler technique, like box breathing or equal breathing.

For those new to breathwork, working with an instructor can provide guidance, support, and a safe space to explore these practices. Remember, this journey is about exploring your breath in a way that feels right for you. Always listen to your body and adjust your practice to suit your personal comfort and needs.

Breathwork for Individuals with a History of Panic Attacks

While breathwork can be an incredibly effective tool for managing stress and processing emotions, it's important to note that certain breathwork techniques may not be suitable for everyone. Just like some medications work well for certain individuals but not for others, more intense breathwork styles, such as those involving rapid or deep breathing, might not be ideal for those with a history of panic attacks. These techniques could potentially amplify feelings of panic.

If you've experienced panic attacks in the past, consider starting with gentler breath techniques. Methods like box breathing, equal breathing, or simply focusing on slow, controlled inhales and exhales can be more soothing and are less likely to trigger heightened anxiety. It's essential to listen to your body and ease into breathwork at a pace that feels comfortable for you.

Additionally, working with a knowledgeable breathwork instructor can provide personalized guidance and support, helping you find the techniques that best suit your needs.

CHAPTER 8
THROUGH DOUBT, TOWARD CALM

"The simple things are also the most extraordinary things, and only the wise can see them." —Paulo Coelho

---

When I first heard about breathwork, I pictured a dim room filled with incense, soft chanting, and vague instructions about "breathing into my third eye." Ponytail optional. I'll be honest—it sounded ridiculous. Breathing was just breathing, something automatic that we all did without thinking. How could it possibly help with real, deep issues like grief, anxiety, or trauma? I brushed it off as another passing wellness trend, the kind of thing that might appeal to someone searching for enlightenment, but not to someone like me, who needed practical solutions.

. . .

If you're reading this and thinking, *Yeah, this all sounds like BS,* I get it. I was right there with you. Breathwork seemed too simple to be effective, too tied up in spiritual jargon to feel relevant to the real world. We live in an age where medical advancements promise quick fixes, where therapy is about talking things through, and where solutions often come packaged in prescriptions. Turning inward and focusing on something as basic as breathing felt counterintuitive. After all, we've been breathing our whole lives—what could possibly be new about it?

Before discovering breathwork, I had explored meditation extensively, even going as far as becoming a certified meditation teacher. I hoped that diving deeper into meditation would help me find the peace and clarity I was seeking. But despite my efforts, meditation never truly clicked for me. Sitting in stillness often felt more like a struggle against my own restless thoughts. I understood its potential benefits, but the practice left me feeling frustrated and disconnected. I kept searching for something that resonated more deeply.

Another doubt that lingered for me—and maybe it does for you too —is the idea that real emotional breakthroughs only happen in the confines of a therapist's office or during some life-altering event. We're conditioned to believe that deep healing requires a structured process, guided by professionals, and punctuated by intense emotional outbursts or profound realizations. The notion that simply sitting and breathing could unlock those same doors felt laughable.

I remember thinking, *Surely, if I needed to work through something as big as grief, I'd need more than this.* But breathwork, as unassuming as it seemed, began to unravel that belief. During one session, without any dramatic buildup, I found myself overwhelmed by a flood of memories and emotions. It wasn't loud or chaotic; it was quiet and steady, like a gentle stream carving its way through stone. I didn't need a therapist's couch or a life crisis to reach that depth—I just needed to breathe.

Pause for a moment. Take a deep breath in through your nose, hold it for a few seconds, and then exhale slowly. Notice how even this small act can shift your awareness, grounding you in the present moment.

One of the first doubts I had, and that many others share, is the simplicity of it all. *How could something so basic make a difference?* It felt almost insulting in its simplicity, like telling someone to just "calm down" during a panic attack. But as I dug deeper into the practice and began to understand the science behind it, my perspective shifted.

Our breath is intimately connected to our nervous system. In moments of stress or fear, our breathing becomes shallow and rapid, triggering the release of stress hormones like cortisol. This physiological response prepares the body to deal with immediate challenges, which can be helpful in genuinely dangerous situations. However, it becomes less beneficial when the stressor is something like a looming deadline or a tough conversation.

Breathwork offers a way to hack this system. By consciously slowing and deepening our breath, we can signal to our body that it's safe, shifting from "fight or flight" to "rest and digest." This isn't just theory; it's backed by research. Studies have shown that deep, controlled breathing can lower heart rate, reduce blood pressure, and decrease cortisol levels. It's a way to regain control when our body feels like it's spiraling out of it.

For someone like me, who spent years trapped in cycles of anxiety, this was a game-changer. I used to think that calming down required a change in circumstances—removing the stressor, fixing the problem. But breathwork taught me that I could create calm within myself, regardless of what was happening externally. It didn't solve all my problems, but it gave me a tool to face them with a clearer, more focused mind.

Another common doubt is the spiritual language often used in breathwork circles. Terms like "energy flow" or "chakra alignment" can feel alien or even off-putting if you're not already inclined toward that kind of thinking. I was wary of it too. I didn't want to chant or visualize beams of light; I just wanted something that worked.

That's where finding the right approach comes in. Not all breathwork practices are steeped in mysticism. There are plenty of teachers who focus on the physiological and psychological benefits without diving into spiritual territory. This practical approach helped me stay engaged, allowing me to experience the benefits without feeling like I had to buy into a belief system that didn't resonate with me.

· · ·

I remember one particular session where my teacher guided us through the basics of diaphragmatic breathing, a technique that focuses on drawing breath deeply into the belly rather than shallowly into the chest. He explained how this method engages the diaphragm, allowing for a fuller, more efficient breath. By breathing this way, we can naturally calm the body and mind, reducing the activation of the stress response. It was fascinating to learn how such a simple shift in how we breathe could have a profound impact on our nervous system. Understanding this made it easier for me to trust the process. It wasn't about believing in something intangible; it was about working with my body's natural rhythm to achieve a sense of balance.

Pause here, and take another deep breath. Let it remind you that even in moments of doubt, there is power in simplicity.

As I continued with breathwork, I began to notice changes not just in how I felt during the sessions, but in my daily life. I became more aware of my reactions to stress and found that I could catch myself before spiraling into anxiety. It was like having a pause button—a moment to step back, breathe, and choose a different response. The more I practiced, the stronger this pause became, allowing me to navigate challenges with greater clarity and calm.

There were still times when I doubted the practice, when I questioned whether it was really making a difference or if it was just a placebo effect. But those doubts became quieter as the evidence of my own experience piled up. I wasn't just calmer; I was more present, more engaged with the world around me. I began to see breathwork not as a cure-all, but as a foundation—a way to ground myself so that I could face life's challenges from a place of stability.

Breathwork taught me that calm isn't something that happens to us; it's something we create. It's a skill, like any other, that gets stronger with practice. And while the idea of sitting and focusing on your breath might seem too simple to be effective, sometimes it's the simplest things that have the greatest impact.

CHAPTER 9
BREATHING THROUGH
THE DARK

Take a deep breath in for four… hold for two… and exhale to the count of six. As you prepare to explore the deep connection between breath and emotions, let each breath center you in the present moment.

There's a unique kind of stillness that comes when you're sitting in the dark, both literally and metaphorically. It's the kind of quiet that can be deafening, filled with the echoes of thoughts you'd rather not face. In those moments, it's easy to feel swallowed by the weight of emotions—grief, fear, anger, or despair. I've been there more times than I'd like to admit. For years, I believed that sitting with those feelings was akin to drowning, and the only way to survive was to fight against them. But breathwork taught me otherwise.

Breathing through the dark is not about escaping the darkness or pretending it doesn't exist. It's about finding a way to sit with it, to breathe into the discomfort, and allow the body and mind to process what's lurking beneath the surface. This wasn't an easy lesson to learn. In fact, it took several sessions before I fully understood the power of simply breathing through my pain rather than fighting it.

I recall one session vividly. The room was dimly lit, and as the guided breathwork began, I felt an overwhelming sense of dread rise within me. My instinct was to stop, to get up and walk away, anything to avoid confronting the feelings that were surfacing. But something told me to stay. With each breath, I focused on expanding my diaphragm, drawing air deeply into my belly, and slowly exhaling. The initial wave of dread began to shift. It didn't disappear, but it softened. What once felt like a tidal wave ready to engulf me now felt more like a steady current, one that I could ride rather than resist.

Breathwork has a way of unlocking deeply buried emotions, often ones we aren't even consciously aware of. These emotions, when unprocessed, can manifest as chronic stress, anxiety, or even physical pain. Breathwork helps to gently release these burdens, creating space for healing and self-awareness.

During that session, I learned that my breath could act as an anchor, a lifeline in the storm. It didn't erase the pain, but it provided a way to navigate it. With each exhale, I released a bit of the tension I had been holding onto for years. It wasn't a dramatic release; there were no sobbing fits or sudden epiphanies. Instead, it was a quiet, steady unraveling—a gradual letting go of the burdens I hadn't realized I was carrying.

• • •

One of the most profound aspects of breathwork is its ability to create space within ourselves. When we're caught in the grip of strong emotions, it can feel like there's no room to breathe, no way out. Breathwork opens up that space, allowing us to step back and observe our emotions without being consumed by them. It teaches us that we can feel deeply without being overwhelmed.

In those dark moments, the simple act of breathing becomes a powerful tool. It's a reminder that no matter how intense the emotions, we have the capacity to sit with them, to breathe through them, and to come out the other side. Breathwork doesn't promise to take away the pain, but it offers a way to coexist with it, to find peace in the midst of chaos.

Research has shown that regular breathwork practice can reduce symptoms of depression and anxiety. It helps regulate the body's stress hormones, bringing the system back into balance. This isn't just about feeling calmer; it's about building resilience, the ability to weather life's storms without being knocked off course.

As I continued my breathwork journey, I noticed that the darkness didn't feel as suffocating as it once did. The same feelings that used to paralyze me now felt manageable. I could acknowledge my grief, sit with my fear, and breathe through my anger. It wasn't that these emotions disappeared; they were still there, but they no longer controlled me. Breathwork had given me the tools to navigate them with a sense of calm and clarity I hadn't known was possible.

• • •

Now, I embrace the dark. There's a strange comfort in knowing that those shadowy corners of my mind no longer scare me. In fact, I get excited when it's time to put on my eyemask and headphones. I know that each session is an opportunity—a chance to dive deep, explore the unknown, and come out stronger, lighter, and more grounded. The darkness has become a familiar companion, and with each breath, I find myself more at peace with it.

What's remarkable is how this practice has rippled into other areas of my life. I find myself approaching challenges with a calmer demeanor, able to pause and breathe rather than react impulsively. My relationships have grown deeper as I've become more present, more willing to listen and engage without the haze of unresolved emotions clouding my mind.

Even creativity flows more freely. After a powerful session, ideas seem to come effortlessly, as if the mental clutter has been swept away, leaving room for clarity and inspiration. This sense of lightness, of being unburdened, stays with me long after the session ends.

What makes breathwork stand out even more is how it compares to meditation. While meditation often involves sitting quietly and attempting to still the mind, I've found that heading into a breathwork session is much more dynamic and engaging. Meditation can sometimes feel like a struggle, especially when the mind refuses to quiet down. Breathwork, on the other hand, harnesses the body's natural rhythm, providing an active process that guides you through the turbulence. There's an energy in breathwork that keeps you connected, a physicality that pulls you deeper. The excitement of knowing I'll be actively working through emotions and sensations makes it a practice I look forward to, rather than one I have to discipline myself to do.

Breathing through the dark has become not just a tool for coping, but a ritual of renewal. Each session is a reminder that no matter how deep the darkness, there is always light waiting to emerge. And with every breath, I'm reminded of the strength I carry within —a strength that grows with each journey inward, lighting the path ahead.

CHAPTER 10

THE COST OF HOLDING ON

For years, I didn't realize how much of my life was shaped by the things I hadn't dealt with. When you're carrying grief and trauma, it doesn't just sit quietly in the back of your mind—it finds ways to weave itself into the choices you make, the people you keep at arm's length, and the stories you tell yourself about who you are. When my brother died, I never consciously decided to build walls around myself, but looking back, that's exactly what I did.

As a kid, I didn't have the words to describe what I was feeling, and even if I did, I wasn't sure anyone would understand. So instead, I kept busy. I got good at being the funny one, the person who could lighten the mood with a quick joke or a sarcastic remark. I didn't see it as avoiding my emotions; I saw it as staying strong. And in a family that valued resilience, it felt like the right thing to do.

But it doesn't always have to be the loss of a loved one. Trauma comes in many forms—bad relationships, school bullying, difficult family dynamics, or anything that leaves a lasting mark on our minds. Sometimes the worst wounds are the ones we don't talk about. And in the internet age, it's easy to avoid those hard feelings. Just like everyone else, I can scroll endlessly or dive into YouTube videos to keep my mind from being too quiet. Those distractions might seem harmless, but they keep us all from being with ourselves.

When I first heard about breathwork, I'll be honest—I thought it sounded like BS. After all, it's just breathing, right? I was skeptical that something so basic could have such a powerful effect. It seemed too simple, almost too easy, to make a real difference. But over time, I began to realize that part of the problem was that we've lost our primal connection to our breath and our minds. We breathe automatically without ever really paying attention to it, without noticing how it affects us mentally and emotionally.

In today's world, where everything is always moving and we're always connected, it's easy to forget that the breath is our most direct link to our nervous system. It's the simplest and most immediate way to calm our bodies and quiet our minds. But because it seems so basic, it's easy to overlook its importance. And because we've lost that connection, it takes more effort to relearn what used to come naturally to us.

During breathwork sessions, I've seen people release emotions they didn't even know they were carrying. I've seen someone start laughing uncontrollably, only to realize that they hadn't felt joy like that in years. I've seen others break down into tears, not knowing why at first, but discovering that they had been holding onto old wounds for decades. There was one person who shared how a breathwork session brought back a forgotten memory of childhood happiness, which made them realize how long it had been since they had felt truly free.

These experiences aren't rare—in fact, they're common. Breathwork creates a space where emotions, memories, and feelings have room to surface without judgment. For me, breathwork helped me see that the death of my brother, while painful, wasn't the only weight I was carrying. Over time, that loss had faded, but it had also become an anchor—a point in my life that other painful experiences clung to like a magnet. I didn't realize it back then, but the grief I felt as a child became a template for how I dealt with every other setback or hardship that followed. It was as if that loss created a pattern in my mind, and everything that came after found its place in that pattern.

One of the hardest things about carrying old grief is that it doesn't show up in obvious ways. It doesn't knock on your door and announce itself; it sneaks in quietly and influences the little things. It's the feeling of restlessness that keeps you from sitting still, the way your stomach tightens when someone asks how you're really doing, or the way you keep finding new distractions to avoid being alone with your thoughts.

Looking back, I can see how those distractions kept piling up. I stayed busy, filled every spare moment with work, hobbies, and projects. And while it seemed like I was just being productive, what I was really doing was running from the silence. The quiet moments were the hardest because that's when the memories had room to come to the surface. It was easier to keep moving, to keep my mind occupied, than to face what was waiting in the stillness.

There were times when my social anxiety felt like a heavy weight I couldn't shake. It wasn't always about big, dramatic moments—sometimes it was something as simple as not knowing what to say in a conversation or worrying that I might say the wrong thing. Even responding to a text message could feel overwhelming. I would open the message, stare at it, and then close my phone because the thought of replying felt like too much. I wasn't just afraid of saying the wrong thing; I was afraid of being seen.

The breakthrough with breathwork was the first time I truly saw the cost of holding on. For so many years, I had convinced myself that the past didn't really matter—that I had moved on, that I was strong enough to keep going. But breathwork forced me to confront the reality that I hadn't moved on. I had just buried the pain under layers of distraction and humor. And in that stillness, I could finally see what I had been running from all along.

Becoming aware of the walls I had built didn't mean I tore them down right away. Healing isn't a switch you can flip, and awareness is only the first step. But that awareness gave me a new perspective on my life and my choices. I started to see that the way I kept people at a distance wasn't just about being "independent" or "easygoing"—it was about protecting myself from the risk of feeling vulnerable. And once I saw that, I knew I had a choice. I could keep living behind those walls, or I could start taking them down, piece by piece.

It wasn't an easy process, and there were times when I doubted whether it was worth it. But I kept going because I had finally tasted what it felt like to live without those walls, even if only for a moment, and I wanted more of that.

What I learned from breathwork is that healing doesn't have to be complicated, but it does require honesty. It means admitting that sometimes we're not okay, and that's alright. It's easy to think that something as simple as breathing can't really help, but it's not just about the act itself—it's about reconnecting to something deeper within ourselves. We breathe to survive, but intentional breathing helps us truly live.

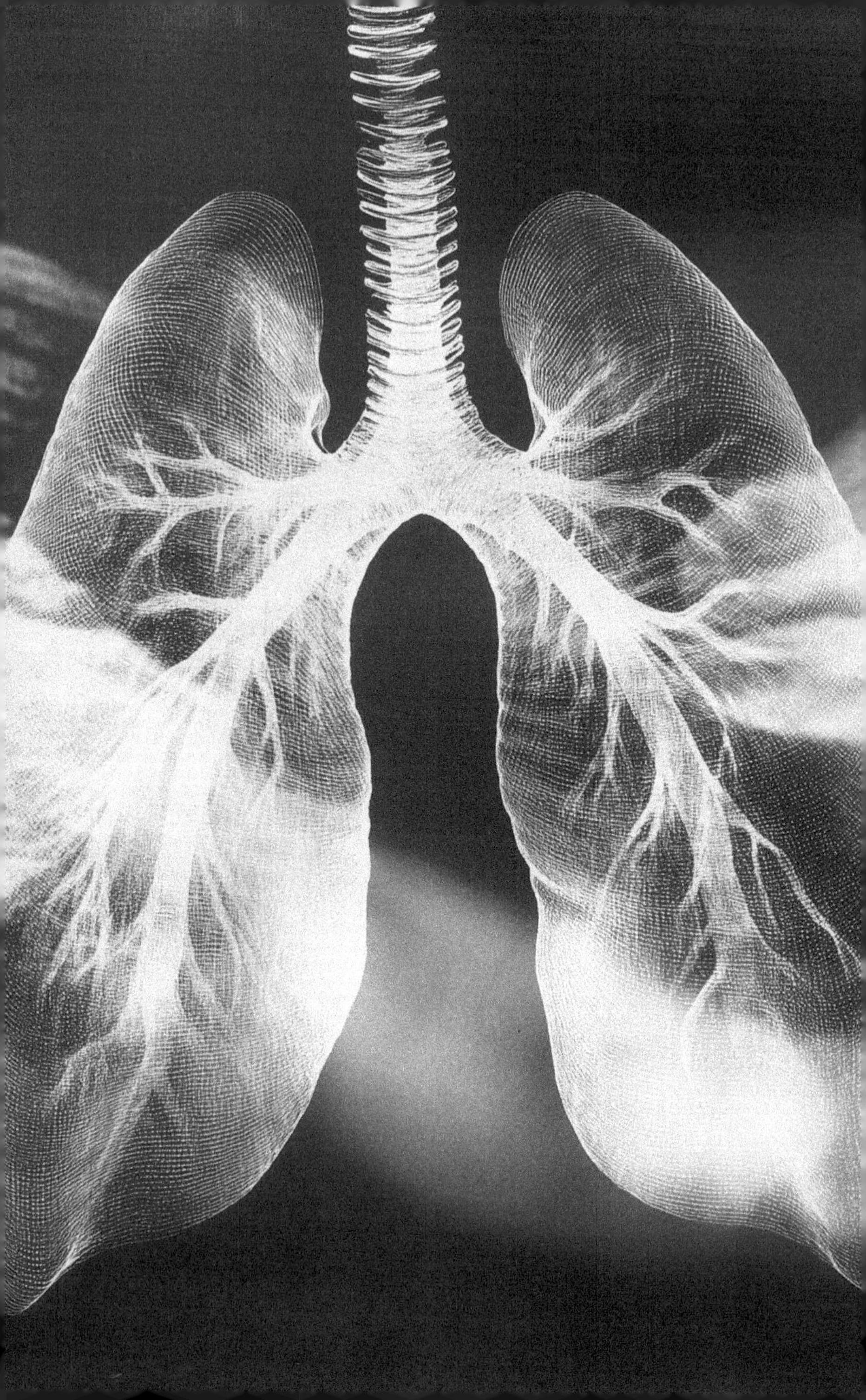

CHAPTER 11
HOW BREATH MOVES THE BODY

What if the way you breathe could immediately shift the chemistry of your body, calming your mind or energizing you in moments?

This isn't some abstract wellness claim—it's a fact rooted in the very mechanics of our physiology. Each breath you take is more than just air filling your lungs; it's a signal, a communication system that influences everything from your heart rate to your emotional state.

Imagine standing on the edge of a cliff, heart racing, breath quickening. Now, think of the deep, slow inhale you take when lying in bed after a long day, feeling your body melt into relaxation. These aren't just reactions—they're your body's way of responding to your breath. Your breath acts like a switchboard, connecting your nervous system, brain, and body in ways science is only beginning to fully understand.

· · ·

This chapter may feel like it's getting a bit in the weeds compared to the rest, but bear with me. When we're skeptical about something new, diving into the science can help justify giving it a shot. Breathwork might sound too simple to be powerful, but understanding how it interacts with our body's systems can shed some light on why it works. We're about to unpack the science behind breathwork—what it's doing under the hood, so to speak—and explore why a simple breath can be a powerful tool for healing.

One of the first steps in breathwork is consciously acknowledging your breath—something we rarely do in our busy lives. We often go through the day without ever noticing our breathing, even though it's with us every moment. Simply taking a moment to observe your own breath is a small but powerful shift. By paying attention to it, you reconnect with something fundamental, becoming more aware of how each inhale and exhale influences your body and mind. This awareness lays the foundation for using the breath as a tool, helping us override stress signals and guide ourselves toward calm.

To understand how breathwork influences the body, we need to start with the nervous system, which has two primary branches. The first is the sympathetic nervous system—often called the "fight-or-flight" response. When we encounter stress, this system kicks into gear, releasing a cascade of hormones like adrenaline and cortisol to prepare us for action. This is a survival response, hardwired from our earliest ancestors who needed to react quickly to dangers in their environment. However, in today's world, stressors are less often physical threats and more likely to be work pressures, family dynamics, or the constant pull of digital distractions.

While the sympathetic response can be life-saving in emergencies, staying in this heightened state can be damaging. Chronic stress, or prolonged activation of the sympathetic nervous system, keeps our bodies on high alert, even when there's no immediate threat. Over time, this "always-on" state can lead to symptoms like anxiety, irritability, fatigue, and weakened immune function. That's where breathwork comes in.

Breathwork allows us to tap into the parasympathetic nervous system, the body's "rest-and-digest" mode. This system is responsible for calming us down, slowing our heart rate, and enabling our bodies to return to a state of balance. When we breathe slowly and deeply, we signal to the parasympathetic nervous system that it's safe to relax. By using breathwork to engage this response, we're giving our bodies a chance to reset, releasing tension and restoring resilience.

One of the key players in this calming response is the vagus nerve, the longest cranial nerve in the body. This nerve connects the brain to many major organs, including the heart, lungs, and digestive system. It serves as a two-way communication line, helping to regulate essential functions like heart rate, breathing, and digestion.

When we engage in deep, slow breathing, we activate the vagus nerve, which, in turn, reduces the production of stress hormones. This helps the body shift from a high-stress mode to a relaxed state. Activating the vagus nerve through breathwork has been shown to lower cortisol levels, reduce inflammation, and increase levels of the neurotransmitter GABA, which promotes calm and well-being. Some studies even suggest that regular activation of the vagus nerve may improve heart health and reduce anxiety.

One of the ways breathwork impacts the vagus nerve is by shifting the balance between inhaling and exhaling. Longer exhales have a unique effect on the nervous system compared to longer inhales. When we exhale for a longer count than we inhale, we create a calming effect by activating the vagus nerve, which signals to the body that it's safe to relax. This practice, often called "parasympathetic breathing," tells the body to release tension and downregulate stress responses. For example, breathing in to a count of four and out to a count of six or eight has been shown to lower heart rate, reduce blood pressure, and ease the mind.

In contrast, longer inhales can have a stimulating effect. By emphasizing the inhale, we engage the sympathetic nervous system, which can help us feel more energized and alert. This approach may be helpful in situations where we need to wake up or focus, but it can increase stress levels if used excessively or in moments when the body craves calm. The balance between inhales and exhales can be a powerful tool, allowing us to tap into our nervous system's natural rhythm, calming or energizing ourselves as needed.

Knowing this, breathwork techniques that emphasize longer exhales are particularly effective for managing stress and anxiety. Through these exercises, we're not just breathing; we're guiding the body into a state of relaxation by harnessing the power of the vagus nerve and allowing our breath to do what it was designed to —restore balance and resilience.

Breath-focused practices aren't new; they span cultures and have been foundational in many traditional healing systems around the world. In ancient India, Pranayama, or the practice of controlled breathing, is a core component of yoga. Pranayama teaches techniques to direct energy, balance the mind, and control the body's natural rhythms. Indian sages recognized thousands of years ago what science is confirming today: that breath is directly tied to our mental and physical states.

Similarly, Taoist breathing techniques in China focus on cultivating and balancing qi, or life energy. Taoist practices emphasize slow, deep breathing that coordinates with movement, as seen in Tai Chi and Qigong. These practices, still popular today, aim to cultivate balance and harmony, reinforcing the idea that our breath connects us to both inner and outer worlds.

Indigenous cultures also recognize the healing power of breath. Native American traditions often include breathing exercises as part of spiritual practices, rituals, and medicine. Breath is viewed as a sacred connection to life and nature, a means of attuning to the world and one's own spirit. Many traditional Indigenous healing practices involve rhythmic breathing to help individuals enter a meditative state or reconnect with their surroundings.

Inhale deeply, filling your lungs… and exhale fully. Allow this breath to remind you of the calming power you hold within each inhale and exhale.

By understanding breathwork's role across cultures, we gain a broader perspective on why controlled breathing has endured as a healing tool. These traditions remind us that breath is more than just a biological function; it is a gateway to emotional balance, resilience, and self-awareness. Whether we approach breathwork from a scientific standpoint or through cultural wisdom, the benefits remain universal.

CHAPTER 12
EMBRACING THE GHOST IN THE MACHINE

Letting go of old grief isn't something that happens in a single breath. It's a process, and like most processes, it's messy, unpredictable, and full of setbacks. I used to think that once you let something go, it was gone for good. But what I've learned through breathwork is that letting go isn't about forgetting —it's about creating enough space within yourself to carry both the past and the present without letting one consume the other.

For most of my life, I felt like I was moving through the world with a piece of me missing. It wasn't an obvious feeling, but more like a quiet emptiness that lingered beneath everything I did. I filled that space with humor, distractions, and busyness, but the feeling never really went away. It was only after I began breathwork that I understood why.

In breathwork, there's a concept of the "ghost in the machine" —the idea that our minds and bodies are like complex machines, but there's something intangible within us that makes us human. That "ghost" is our consciousness, our emotions, our sense of self. It's what makes us more than just the sum of our parts. And for a long time, I felt disconnected from that part of myself. I was functioning, but I wasn't really living.

Breathwork didn't just help me process old grief; it helped me reconnect with the parts of myself I had been ignoring. It allowed me to feel the full weight of my experiences without being overwhelmed by them. And in that stillness, I began to see the ways I had been living half a life—always holding back, always afraid of what might happen if I let my guard down.

I've come to realize that we're all navigating a tough world. Every one of us has our own personal reality, shaped by our past experiences, and no two people's realities are the same. This means we all carry different burdens, see things through different lenses, and react to the world in unique ways. But if we can learn to meet ourselves where we are, without judgment, we can begin to shift that reality. It's about retraining our attention and controlling our focus. When we do that, we can start to catch ourselves in those moments of negativity before they spiral out of control.

It's not about eliminating negative thoughts altogether—that's impossible—but about noticing them as they arise, acknowledging their root, and defusing the situation before it becomes a storm. It's like moving from the passenger seat to the driver's seat, where you can steer instead of just being taken for a ride.

The more I've let go of old patterns and started paying attention to my mind, the more I've seen how much of my suffering came from holding on. We live in a world that teaches us to keep adding things—to buy more, to do more, to fill every empty space with something new. There's this cultural groupthink that happiness comes through addition: If you're unhappy, just buy more of this or that. If something is wrong, take another pill. You'll be happy if you can just get one more thing. But that kind of thinking doesn't lead to happiness—it leads to a cluttered life and a cluttered mind.

And when our minds are overwhelmed, our default mode is to suppress what we're feeling instead of getting help. We end up adding pressure to hold down those emotions, pretending they're not there, and that just creates more suffering. Instead, what we need to do is start stripping things away. We need to clear out the clutter from our internal closets, letting go of the things that no longer serve us.

Breathwork taught me that it's not about adding something new—it's about reconnecting to what's already there, beneath all the noise and distractions. It's about finding stillness and allowing ourselves to just be, without constantly striving to be more or do more.

One of the biggest changes I noticed was in the way I related to other people. I used to think that keeping things light and friendly was the best way to avoid getting hurt. But as I started to let go of old patterns, I found myself wanting deeper connections. I wanted to be seen, not just as the funny or easygoing guy, but as a whole person with a full range of emotions.

That desire wasn't comfortable at first. It felt risky, like stepping out onto thin ice. But the more I practiced being open, the more I realized that vulnerability wasn't as scary as I had made it out to be. That's not to say that everything changed overnight. There were still moments when old habits kicked in, when I found myself retreating into humor or deflecting uncomfortable questions. But over time, I became more aware of those patterns, and awareness made it easier to choose a different path. Instead of running from my emotions, I started to sit with them, to breathe through them, and to let them pass without judgment.

It wasn't just my emotions that breathwork helped me reconnect with—it was my sense of purpose. For so long, I had been running on autopilot, going through the motions of life without really engaging with it. Breathwork gave me a new sense of clarity, a reminder that I didn't have to live my life in reaction to the past. I could choose how I wanted to move forward, and I could do it on my own terms.

I think a lot of us go through life feeling like there's a disconnect between who we are and who we want to be. We carry around old wounds, old stories, and old habits that keep us stuck in patterns we don't even realize we're in. And because we're so used to carrying that weight, we don't question whether we can let it go. Breathwork showed me that it's possible to release that weight, but it also taught me that letting go isn't something you do once and forget about. It's a practice, a choice you make over and over again.

In my classes, I've seen people have breakthroughs that mirror my own experiences. Some come in skeptical, not sure what to expect, and leave feeling like a burden has been lifted. Others come in already carrying a lot of pain, and breathwork gives them a safe space to finally feel what they've been holding in. I've seen people cry, laugh, scream, and fall into deep, peaceful silence. It's a reminder that we all have our own ghosts, our own stories, and our own ways of coping with the world.

For me, breathwork isn't just about processing emotions—it's about reconnecting with the "ghost in the machine," the part of me that's more than just the sum of my experiences. It's about finding balance between being vulnerable and being resilient, between holding on and letting go. It's about creating space within myself to carry the past without letting it define me.

Looking back, I can see that the pain of losing my brother was like an anchor that held other experiences in place. It pulled in everything that came after—every hardship, every setback, every unresolved emotion. And for a long time, I thought that anchor was just part of who I was. But breathwork showed me that it didn't have to be. I could choose to carry my brother's memory without letting it weigh me down. I could honor his life without being defined by his death.

In a way, breathwork helped me find a new way to hold onto the past—not as a burden, but as a part of my story that I can carry with compassion and grace. It helped me embrace the "ghost" within me, not as something broken or incomplete, but as a reminder that I'm still here, still breathing, still alive.

CHAPTER 13

INTEGRATING THE PRACTICE

Building new habits isn't easy. I learned this quickly when I first started trying to make breathwork a regular part of my life. I thought it would be as simple as adding another task to my day, like checking off a box on a to-do list. But breathwork doesn't work that way. It's not something you can just cram into an already packed schedule and hope it sticks. And like most new habits, it requires more than just good intentions.

One thing I realized early on is that expecting myself to commit to a full hour of breathwork every day wasn't realistic. Most people don't even find the time for a 15-minute workout, let alone an hour of just breathing. So instead of aiming for long sessions every day, I started with something more manageable: small techniques that I could use whenever I felt myself getting irritated, stressed, or overwhelmed.

For me, one of the most effective techniques was box breathing. It's simple: breathe in for four counts, hold for four counts, exhale for four counts, and then hold again for four counts. This technique became my go-to whenever I found myself in traffic or dealing with everyday frustrations. It didn't take long to notice that these short sessions of controlled breathing could make a big difference in my state of mind. When I felt tension building, I could use a few rounds of box breathing to calm my nerves and regain my focus.

One thing that transformed my breathwork practice was using a pair of noise-canceling headphones and an eye mask during sessions. For me, it's not just about shutting out external distractions; it's about creating an environment where I can go as deep as possible. The headphones block out the noise of daily life, while the eye mask helps remove visual stimuli, making it easier to turn inward.

But what really makes a difference is the music. I've found that the right soundtrack can act as a guide, leading me through the peaks and valleys of a session. Slow, rhythmic tracks help me stay grounded during intense moments, while ambient sounds can pull me into a meditative state where time seems to dissolve. Music is like a current that carries me, and when I'm fully immersed in it, I can let go of the chatter in my mind and just be.

Pro-tip: For your first few sessions, choose instrumental music you're unfamiliar with. Lyrics and attachments to familiar tunes can quickly pull you out of the experience.

If you're trying to deepen your practice, I recommend experimenting with these elements. It doesn't have to be complicated or even spiritual—just find what helps you feel more present and connected to the experience.

But there are plenty of other techniques to try if box breathing doesn't resonate. Here are a few others I've found effective:

1. **4-7-8 Breathing**: Inhale for four counts, hold your breath for seven counts, and exhale slowly for eight counts. This technique is great for winding down before bed or calming down during moments of high anxiety.
2. **Alternate Nostril Breathing**: Close one nostril with your finger, inhale through the other, then switch and exhale through the opposite nostril. It's a simple practice that can help balance your nervous system and clear your mind.
3. **Equal Breathing**: Inhale and exhale for an equal number of counts, such as four or five each. This technique is all about finding a steady rhythm to bring your focus back to the present moment.

While these simple techniques can be incredibly helpful, finding the right coach or guide is also crucial. Breathwork isn't a one-size-fits-all practice, and every teacher has their own methods and philosophy. It's kind of like finding a musician you connect with—some people gravitate toward classic rock, while others find their groove in jazz. In the same way, the breathwork teacher who resonates with you can make all the difference in your practice.

. . .

Here are a few popular types of breathwork you might want to explore:

1. **Holotropic Breathwork**: Developed by Stanislav Grof, this method involves intense, fast breathing to reach altered states of consciousness. It's often done in a group setting with music and is aimed at deep emotional release and self-exploration. It's powerful, but not for the faint of heart.
2. **Pranayama**: This traditional practice from India focuses on controlling the breath to influence the mind and body. Techniques like alternate nostril breathing, Kapalabhati (skull-shining breath), and Ujjayi (victorious breath) fall under this category. It's a foundational practice in yoga and emphasizes balance and discipline.
3. **Wim Hof Method**: This technique combines breathing exercises, cold exposure, and mindset training. The breathing aspect involves a series of deep, controlled breaths followed by breath holds. It's known for boosting resilience, improving focus, and enhancing physical performance.

I encourage you to look into each of these methods and explore which one resonates with you. My personal approach to breathwork is very practical and utilitarian. In my sessions, it's about getting in, breathing, and getting out—no fluff, no mysticism, just the work. That's what works for me, and it's how I structure my classes.

. . .

When it comes to building a breathwork practice, the most important thing is to find what fits your personality and your life. There's no right or wrong way to approach it, just like there's no single way to listen to music. Some people need a more spiritual experience, while others, like me, prefer something straightforward and functional.

By trying different techniques and working with different teachers or guides, you can find what feels right for you. Remember, it's not about doing it perfectly—it's about being open to the experience and finding a practice that helps you stay grounded, focused, and connected to yourself.

Exploring Psychedelic-Assisted Therapy

While breathwork is a powerful tool for healing and self-exploration, it's not the only one out there. Over recent years, there's been a resurgence of interest in psychedelic-assisted therapy. Techniques using substances like ketamine, psilocybin (the active compound in psychedelic mushrooms), and MDMA are showing incredible promise in treating PTSD, depression, anxiety, and other deep-seated emotional traumas.

Psychedelics, when administered in a controlled and therapeutic setting, can create profound experiences. They have the potential to loosen rigid thought patterns and dissolve the walls we build around ourselves, giving people access to deep layers of their subconscious mind. For some, it's like opening a door to past traumas that have been locked away for years, allowing for the processing and release of old wounds in a safe, supported environment.

Ketamine therapy, for example, is legal in many areas and often used to treat severe depression. It works quickly to create a dissociative state, allowing patients to view their problems from a new perspective. Psilocybin and MDMA, while not yet fully legal, are being researched and decriminalized in several regions due to their incredible potential in helping people work through trauma and achieve lasting healing.

But as promising as these therapies are, there are hurdles to consider. Psychedelic-assisted therapy can be expensive and often requires a skilled guide or therapist to administer the treatment safely. There's also a legal grey area around many of these substances, which can make access complicated depending on where you live.

That's one of the reasons I've found breathwork to be such a valuable practice—it's simple, accessible, and doesn't require any external substances. Breathwork can mimic some of the same deep, introspective effects that psychedelics offer, but without the legal concerns or high cost. And while it's not a one-to-one comparison, breathwork gives people a chance to explore their inner landscape and confront difficult emotions in a safe, grounded way.

If you're curious about psychedelic-assisted therapy, I encourage you to do your research and look into the professionals offering these services. They can be life-changing for some people, but breathwork remains a solid foundation for those looking to start exploring their emotions and releasing old pain in a gentle, natural way.

CHAPTER 14
THE RIPPLE EFFECT

Change doesn't happen overnight, and even when it does, it doesn't stay static. It ripples outward, touching every part of your life in ways you don't always expect. Breathwork wasn't a magic solution that suddenly made everything better, but it was a turning point—a moment when I began to live more consciously, more intentionally. And from that point on, the changes didn't just stop with me.

Take a deep breath in for four… hold for two… and exhale for six. Prepare yourself to explore the ripple effect of change and how breathwork influences not just you, but those around you.

For a long time, I carried the weight of unresolved emotions, even when I wasn't aware of it. They lingered beneath the surface, shaping how I interacted with others and how I saw myself. When I finally began to release that weight, it was like clearing away the fog that had been clouding my view. And as that fog lifted, I could see the ripple effect of those changes spreading into different areas of my life.

In relationships, the biggest shift was moving away from

keeping things on the surface. Before, I was friendly and easygoing, always making people laugh but rarely letting anyone see beyond that. Humor was my shield, and it worked well enough to keep people at arm's length. But when I began to acknowledge my own emotions, I found myself wanting deeper connections, even if it meant being uncomfortable at times. I wanted to be seen as more than just the funny guy—I wanted to be seen as a whole person, with all the messiness that came with it.

That desire wasn't easy to embrace. It felt risky, like stepping out onto thin ice. But the more I practiced being open, the more I realized that vulnerability wasn't as dangerous as I had made it out to be. It wasn't about sharing every detail of my life or spilling my guts to everyone I met. It was about being present, being real, and letting go of the need to control how I was perceived. In the past, I might have seen a moment of tension or an uncomfortable silence as something to defuse with a joke. Now, I'm more willing to sit with that discomfort and see what happens.

That doesn't mean I've abandoned humor—it's still a big part of who I am, and I still get a lot of joy out of making people laugh. But it's not the only tool in my toolbox anymore. I've learned that sometimes, it's okay to let the silence hang, to let a moment be what it is without trying to change it.

Breathwork also changed the way I experience creativity. Before, my mind was always racing, full of distractions and unfinished thoughts. I struggled to find focus, to cut through the noise and get to the heart of what I wanted to express. But as I practiced breathwork, I found that it created a space in my mind that wasn't there before. It was like clearing out a cluttered room, making room for new ideas to flow in. After a strong session, I often felt like my creativity was on overdrive—ideas would come to me in a rush, and I'd feel a sense of clarity that I hadn't experienced before.

One of the most unexpected benefits of breathwork was how it deepened my connection to nature. Walks in the woods had always been a way to clear my head, but now they felt different. It was as if I had unlocked a new layer of awareness, one that allowed me to experience the world more fully. The sounds of the forest, the feel of the breeze on my skin, the way the light filtered through the leaves—everything felt more vivid, more alive. It wasn't just about being in nature; it was about being present with myself in that space.

Breathwork helped me reconnect with a part of myself that I had been ignoring for a long time. It showed me that I wasn't defined by my past or by the roles I had tried to play. I wasn't just the funny guy, or the person who kept everyone at a distance. I was more than that, and I didn't need to fit into anyone else's expectations.

That shift in perspective made it easier to relate to others. I wasn't constantly worried about how I was being perceived, or whether I was saying the "right" thing. I could just be myself, and trust that the people who mattered would accept me for who I was. That doesn't mean I'm suddenly an open book or that I've let go of all my old habits. I'm still a bit standoffish at times, but that's just part of who I am. The difference now is that I understand it, and I can accept it without feeling like it's something I need to fix.

Looking back, I can see how all these small changes have added up over time. Breathwork didn't just help me let go of old grief—it helped me let go of the need to be perfect, to always have it all figured out. It taught me to embrace the messiness of life, to be okay with not having all the answers. And in doing so, it gave me the freedom to be more present, more patient, and more open to whatever came my way.

The funny thing about change is that it doesn't always announce itself with a big fanfare. Sometimes, it sneaks up on you, revealing itself in small, quiet moments. It's the way you handle a difficult conversation without feeling defensive, or the way you let go of a grudge that used to eat at you. It's the way you find yourself sitting in silence without feeling the need to fill it, or the way you feel more at peace with who you are, flaws and all.

For me, breathwork was the catalyst for those changes. It didn't fix everything or erase the past, but it gave me a new way to approach the present. It showed me that healing isn't a destination —it's a journey, one that requires patience, persistence, and a willingness to be uncomfortable. And as I continue to walk that path, I can see the ripple effect of those changes spreading outward, touching every part of my life in ways I never expected.

CHAPTER 15
SEEING THROUGH THE LENS OF BREATHWORK

Breathwork changed the way I perceive the world and others around me. It's like each breathwork session tilts the lens just enough to let you glimpse behind the curtain of someone's behavior, to see the old patterns and facades that they've built to protect themselves. Understanding this made me realize that, despite my attempts to avoid it, my brother's death didn't just mark a moment in my past—it colored everything that came after it.

Breathwork taught me to look deeper at people, to see the vulnerable, hurting child still within each of us, trying to navigate a world that often feels hostile or indifferent. It helped me see that, in many ways, we're all still dealing with old wounds, each of us trying to find ways to protect ourselves from the things that scared us when we were young.

I now have two sons of my own, and in a strange twist of fate, they're almost ten years apart—just like my brother and me. The symmetry isn't lost on me, and it's a reminder of how cycles seem to repeat themselves, even when we're not paying attention. Raising them has been a journey that's both joyful and humbling, and it's made me reflect even more deeply on my relationship with my brother and what it means to be the one who's still here.

Living a few hours away from my parents now, I often think about what's changed and what hasn't. My parents don't live in the same house anymore, but they stayed on the same property. That land has a way of holding memories, even as time moves on. Visiting them, I'm reminded of the spaces where we shared laughter, where we grieved, and where life continued in the midst of pain. I see my boys running around the same hills and woods that my brother and I explored together, and sometimes it feels like time hasn't really moved at all. It's like a thread connecting the past to the present, weaving all of these moments together.

I can still hear certain songs or smell familiar scents that instantly bring tears to my eyes when they remind me of my brother. But those tears aren't just about the pain anymore—they're about the connection to his memory, a way to keep a piece of him alive within me. I've come to welcome those moments because they're not about reliving the loss—they're about honoring what was. I adore those memories and will forever be grateful for each one of them, no matter how small.

Having my own children has also made me more aware of how early experiences shape who we become. I feel for children who experience horrific things because I know firsthand how those events can linger and leave an impact. As adults, we're often just grown-up versions of the kids we once were, carrying old wounds into new relationships and situations. Breathwork helped me understand that, and it made me realize that we're all just trying to make sense of the world with the tools we were given.

Even now, I'm still a no-nonsense, "manly" man in many ways, but I've come to acknowledge the power of feelings and emotions. I've learned that understanding and embracing them isn't a sign of weakness—it's a sign of strength. It's about being human, about being present in the messy, beautiful reality of life.

CHAPTER 16

A MESSAGE TO THOSE STILL SEARCHING

f you're reading this, there's a good chance you've been through some tough times. You might be carrying around a weight that feels impossible to describe, or you've experienced things you can't quite let go of. Maybe you've felt like there's a part of you that's stuck, or that old memories have a grip on your life in ways you don't fully understand. And if you've gotten this far, it means you haven't given up trying to find some kind of answer—something to make it all make sense or, at the very least, make it easier to bear.

I want to talk to you directly, the person who feels like they've tried everything, or maybe someone who doesn't even know where to start. Whether it's grief, trauma, stress, or anxiety that's weighing on you, there's something I've learned through my own journey that I want to share. And that's this: healing doesn't have to be complicated or reserved for people with the right credentials. It's not some distant goal or something that only experts can hand down to you. Sometimes, it's as simple as sitting down and breathing through the pain.

That might sound strange at first. After all, breathing is something we do every day without a second thought. But what if that breath could be a bridge—one that connects the chaos inside you to a place of peace? What if those breaths could help you let go of old patterns, old pain, and the old stories you keep telling yourself about who you are and what you can or can't do?

I came to breathwork after hearing about it in meditation chats and from books. At the time, I didn't really understand what it could do for me. I just knew I needed something to change. And even though I was skeptical, I gave it a try. During my breakthrough, it was like a huge weight was lifted from deep within me —a weight I didn't even realize was there. I felt true love, joy, and peace all at once, almost like reconnecting with a part of myself I had forgotten.

Pause here and breathe deeply, allowing your breath to flow naturally. Acknowledge the weight you may be carrying, letting this breath remind you that you're not alone in your struggles.

What's most surprising is that breathwork isn't religious in nature. It's not about subscribing to a specific belief system, but it does have a way of bringing you closer to whatever higher power you believe in. Whether that's God, the universe, or just a deeper sense of self, the connection becomes clearer. It's like sailing instead of rowing—allowing yourself to move with the current instead of fighting against it.

So, if you're carrying social anxiety, grief, trauma, or just feel like you're spinning your wheels in stress, I encourage you to give it a try. Start small, maybe by following a YouTube video or reaching out to me if you want some guidance. Just keep in mind that it might take a few sessions before you feel the shift. It did for me, and it does for many others. But the changes can be profound and life-changing.

One of the biggest obstacles is the doubt that creeps in—the expectation that real solutions only come from authority figures like doctors in pill form or therapists with degrees. While there's nothing wrong with seeking help from professionals, don't under-estimate the power of what you can do for yourself. You don't need fancy tools or expensive treatments to start healing. All you need is your breath, your focus, and a willingness to show up for yourself.

I know it can be easy to settle into hopelessness, to think that things won't change or that what you're feeling is just something you have to live with. But I want you to know that you don't have to settle. There are always options, and hope is real. Breathwork isn't a cure-all, but it's a start, and sometimes that's all you need to find a new path.

If you're struggling, don't be afraid to reach out for help, and don't be afraid to try something new. Healing isn't a straight line, and it doesn't look the same for everyone. But the most important thing is to keep moving forward, even if it's one small breath at a time. You've got this. And if you need a reminder, just take a deep breath, let it out, and remember that you're stronger than you think. Stay open to the process, stay curious, and keep going. The road ahead isn't always easy, but it's worth every step.

CHAPTER 17
THREE-DAY BREATH IMMERSION

Congratulations on reaching this point, and thank you for spending this time with me. Throughout these chapters, we've explored how breathwork can help release trauma, reclaim attention, and discover calm within. Now, it's time to engage with it firsthand. This Three-Day Breath Immersion offers a simple but impactful way to connect with your breath and put the practices you've learned into daily action.

These three days will introduce you to approachable breathwork techniques that you can use anytime for calm and connection. Think of them as daily maintenance—ways to keep your mind clear and your body grounded. If you're curious about a deeper experience, breathwork sessions with an instructor offer an even more powerful approach.

My classes are like a workout for your mind and body. They involve forceful breathing for up to 30 minutes, creating a transformative, "deep-cleaning" experience that's ideal for releasing old tension or stuck emotions. While they're intense, almost anyone can do them, and they don't have to be done as often, though some choose to practice weekly. This three-day challenge is a great way to integrate breathwork daily, but know that a guided class can take you to an even deeper place.

So, let's dive into this immersion. Each day, take a few minutes to breathe, connect, and let go. After each session, use the provided journaling prompts to capture your reflections and solidify your experience.

Preparing for the Immersion

Before you begin, here are a few steps to help make the most of your experience:

1. **Create Your Space:** Find a quiet spot where you won't be interrupted. It could be a cozy corner, a room with natural light, or anywhere you feel comfortable.

2. **Turn Off Distractions:** Silence your phone, turn off notifications, and minimize anything that might pull your focus away from the practice.

3. **Set an Intention:** Take a moment to reflect on why you're doing this immersion. Perhaps it's to find calm, connect with yourself, or simply explore the practice of breathwork.

Think of each day as a small ritual, a few dedicated minutes to connect with yourself through the breath. When you're ready, let's begin.

Day 1: Awareness & Connection

Objective: Begin with awareness, reconnecting with the natural rhythm of your breath. This day is about noticing the subtleties of your breath and the impact of simple awareness on your state of mind.

1. **Find Your Breath:** Sit comfortably, placing one hand on your belly and one on your chest. Close your eyes if you're comfortable doing so.

2. **Observe:** Spend 5 minutes observing your breath without trying to change it. Notice if it's shallow or deep, fast or slow.

3. **Diaphragmatic Breathing:** After a few minutes, start deepening the breath, allowing your belly to rise with each inhale. Count to 4 as you inhale, then exhale for 4, feeling the breath in your belly.

Reflection and Journaling:
Take a few moments after this practice to write about what you observed. Did any emotions or sensations surface? Sometimes the subtlest feelings—like a sense of peace or underlying tension—can reveal a lot.

Journaling Prompt: "Today, as I focused on my breath, I noticed…"

• • •

Tips: If your mind wanders, gently bring your focus back to the feeling of your breath under your hands. Think of this as tuning in to a quieter frequency in your mind.

Day 2: Control & Calm

Objective: Develop a sense of calm by practicing control over your breath's pace. Today's exercise, Box Breathing, is simple yet powerfully calming.

1. **Find Your Space:** Sit or lie comfortably, and take a few deep breaths to settle.

2. **Box Breathing:** Inhale for 4 counts, hold for 4, exhale for 4, and hold again for 4.

3. **Repeat:** Continue this pattern for 5 minutes, focusing on making each part of the breath cycle equal.

Reflection and Journaling:

Write down how Box Breathing affected you. Did slowing down create any sense of calm or control in your body or mind? Sometimes, this exercise can reveal hidden tension or a surprising calm.

Journaling Prompt: "When I slow my breath, I notice…"

Optional Reflection: Think about any situations in life where slowing down could help you regain control or clarity. This journaling can be a powerful way to connect your breathwork practice to everyday moments.

. . .

Tips: If you feel tense during the breath holds, reduce the count to 3 or even 2 seconds. Box Breathing is a favorite of first responders and athletes for a reason—it's simple, steady, and calming.

Day 3: Depth & Release

Objective: Slow and lengthen the breath, creating a release from tension and inviting deeper relaxation. Today's exercise, 4-7-8 Breathing, naturally reduces anxiety and deepens presence.

1. **Prepare for Calm:** Find a quiet space and take a few centering breaths.

2. **4-7-8 Breathing:** Inhale through your nose for 4, hold for 7, and exhale slowly through your mouth for 8. Repeat for 5-10 minutes.

3. **Let Go:** Focus on the lengthened exhale and let any remaining tension melt away with each breath.

Reflection and Journaling:

This is your opportunity to reflect on the practice of release. What sensations or thoughts surfaced as you practiced 4-7-8 Breathing? Were there any emotions or memories that felt like they loosened their grip?

Journaling Prompt: "With each breath, I let go of…"

. . .

Optional Reflection: Consider any areas in life where you're holding on too tightly—whether to stress, relationships, or expectations. Let your breathwork practice help you begin to release these, one breath at a time.

Tips: If 4-7-8 Breathing feels intense, start by holding for 4 or 5 instead of 7. Focus on the long exhale, letting it draw out the tension from your day.

After the Immersion: Moving Forward

Congratulations on completing the Three-Day Breath Immersion. This immersion offers just a glimpse into what's possible with breathwork. Take a moment to appreciate your effort, and know that each technique you've practiced is a tool you can carry forward.

While this immersion provides a solid foundation, a full one-hour session with an instructor can offer a whole new level of experience. Think of it like going to the gym alone versus working with a personal trainer. In a self-led session, you're familiar with the techniques and get a good mental and emotional "workout." But with an instructor, it's like having that personal trainer guiding you through a session. They encourage you to push past your usual limits, show you new techniques, and help you explore layers of yourself you might not reach on your own. Under their guidance, you can access a depth of emotional release, clarity, and mental stillness that a self-led session may only touch upon. It's an experience that can feel transformative, like a full "reset" that leaves you lighter, more grounded, and more open.

. . .

Journaling Reflection: Now that you've completed the immersion, reflect on any shifts you've noticed, whether physical, emotional, or mental. What insights did this experience bring to the surface?

Journaling Prompt: "After three days of breathwork, I feel…"

Suggestions for Integrating Breathwork:

• **Combine Techniques:** Mix and match the techniques as needed. Try Box Breathing during a stressful workday or 4-7-8 before bed.
   • **Daily Reminders:** Practice mindful breaths throughout the day, even if it's just a few seconds of deep belly breathing.
   • **Track Your Journey:** Notice any shifts in your mental state over time as you incorporate these exercises into your routine.

Final Thoughts

This immersion is just the beginning. Think of each technique as a way to reset, reconnect, and recalibrate. Let each breath remind you of the peace and resilience within, and know that the journey you've started can continue to unfold in meaningful ways. For those looking to experience the true depth of breathwork, a guided one-hour session offers the kind of intensity and transformative release that can open doors to emotions and insights lying just beneath the surface. A class with an instructor is a chance to go beyond routine and experience the real impact of breathwork, creating space for clarity, healing, and calm.

. . .

Take a deep breath in for four…and exhale for eight. This is where healing begins.

CHAPTER 18

STARTING TOOLKIT FOR BREATHWORK

Breathwork is simple—it only requires you, your breath, and a bit of quiet. But a few helpful tools can make the experience even richer. Here's my "Starting Toolkit," designed for any budget and put together with a flexible, low-pressure approach.

As a thank you for exploring the power of breathwork through this book, I'm offering you 50% off your first class with me. Use the coupon code **BREATHDEEP** when booking your session at www.-mutethemind.com. This is a great opportunity to dive deeper into your practice with guided support.

For the most updated and more extensive recommendations, many of which are regularly updated, visit www.mutethemind.com/tools.

Comfort Tools

Creating a comfortable setting makes it easier to relax and

focus, especially in the beginning. Here are a few items that help eliminate distractions:

- **Manta Ray Eye Mask ($35)** – This blackout eye mask helps block out light and lets you dive deeper into your practice. If you're on a budget, a simple sleep mask or even a soft scarf can work just as well.
- **Yoga or Meditation Mat ($10-$50)** – If you're practicing on a hard floor, a mat adds some much-needed padding. Choose one that feels comfortable to you—most budget-friendly options will work. And if you're improvising, even a blanket or rug will do in a pinch!
- **Journal (Free-$20)** – A simple journal can be invaluable for jotting down thoughts, feelings, or reflections after your sessions. Tracking your experiences can help you notice patterns and progress over time.

Sound Enhancement

Sound can be a powerful tool in breathwork. Good-quality headphones, combined with calming music, help create a focused environment and drown out external distractions.

- **Noise-Canceling Headphones**:
  - *Sony MX4 ($250)* – High-quality, immersive headphones for a completely distraction-free experience.
  - *Anker Q20 ($40)* – A budget-friendly option that still provides solid noise cancellation.

Tip: Use these with your favorite relaxing playlist on Spotify or a guided breathwork session on YouTube for a truly immersive experience.

. . .

Free Tools

Breathwork is about simplicity, so there are plenty of free resources to help you get started. Here are some great options:

• **Spotify and YouTube Playlists** – Plenty of playlists are designed for breathwork, with calming tones and rhythms that naturally guide your breathing. Try searching "breathwork playlist" on either platform, and feel free to explore until you find tracks that resonate with you.

• **DIY Substitutions** – You don't need high-end items to make breathwork effective. Substitute a folded towel for a mat or use any type of headphones with calming music to create an easy, inexpensive setup.

Practical Tips for Using Your Toolkit

Once you have your toolkit ready, here are a few tips for making the most of it:

• **Set Up a Quiet Space** – Whether you're at home or on the go, find a spot with minimal interruptions.

• **Combine Tools for Full Effect** – Use your eye mask and headphones together with a guided playlist for a deeper session, especially if you're in a noisy or busy environment.

• **Start Small** – Explore with whatever you have available, and build up only if you feel it enhances your practice. Remember, breathwork is about you and your focus—not about equipment.

Final Thoughts

Breathwork doesn't require anything fancy. The beauty of this practice is in its accessibility and simplicity. Use this Starting Toolkit if it feels right, but remember that your breath alone is the real tool. Breathe, relax, and let this practice work for you, no matter what you have around you.

CHAPTER 19
THE NEXT BREATH

As you close this book, take a moment to pause. You've taken in new ideas, explored your breath, and maybe even uncovered something unexpected along the way.

Take a deep breath in through your nose to the count of four— feel the air filling your lungs, expanding your chest, making space.

Hold for a brief moment, allowing this sense of fullness to settle.

Now, exhale slowly to the count of eight—let the breath flow out naturally, releasing any tension, and feel a quiet calm as it leaves your body.

As you breathe, let yourself be present in this moment, without expectation. Just here, just breathing. Take in the simplicity, the peace, and remember: this feeling is yours, whenever you need it.

ABOUT THE AUTHOR

Jody Elliott grew up in rural Kentucky, navigating life with humor and a quiet resilience shaped by early loss. A self-described skeptic with social anxiety, Jody discovered the power of breathwork after a series of failed attempts, finding a deep sense of peace and clarity in moments of stillness. Today, he teaches others how to use simple techniques to work through grief, anxiety, and the distractions of a busy world. When not writing or teaching, Jody enjoys spending time with his family, taking quiet walks in nature, and sharing a laugh with those around him.

If you're interested in doing breathwork sessions with Jody, visit www.mutethemind.com.